Fighting Fate

Justin Yerbury

16pt

Copyright Page from the Original Book

First published by Affirm Press in 2023
Boon Wurrung Country
28 Thistlethwaite Street
South Melbourne VIC 3205
affirmpress.com.au

10 9 8 7 6 5 4 3 2 1

Text copyright © Justin Yerbury, 2023
Images copyright © Justin and Rachel Yerbury unless otherwise stated
All rights reserved. No part of this publication may be reproduced without prior written permission from the publisher.

 A catalogue record for this book is available from the National Library of Australia

Cover design by Luke Causby / Blue Cork © Affirm Press
Cover image © Paul Jones / University of Wollongong

TABLE OF CONTENTS

Foreword	iv
Foreword	viii
Author's Note	xi
Prologue	xiii
Chapter One: Golden Days	1
Chapter Two: A New Orbit	18
Chapter Three: Storm Clouds on the Horizon	31
Chapter Four: A Strange Relationship with Death	40
Chapter Five: Winter Within	54
Chapter Six: The Work Begins	63
Chapter Seven: The Promise	80
Chapter Eight: The Unwelcome Member of the Family	90
Chapter Nine: Our World Crumbling Once More	102
Chapter Ten: The Clock Starts Ticking	116
Chapter Eleven: Cambridge	120
Chapter Twelve: Prions	137
Chapter Thirteen: A Fantastical Submarine World	152
Chapter Fourteen: Hyperexcitability and Darkness	165
Chapter Fifteen: The Beast Closes In	177
Chapter Sixteen: Looking for Hope	187
Chapter Seventeen: The Year of Lasts	198
Chapter Eighteen: My Own Personal Black Hole	213
Chapter Nineteen: Into the Twilight	224
Acknowledgements	243
Notes and Resources	246
Back Cover Material	274

TABLE OF CONTENTS

Foreword ... v
Foreword ... viii
Author's Note ... ix
Prologue ... xiii
Chapter One: Golden Days ... 1
Chapter Two: A New Cabin ... 16
Chapter Three: Storm Clouds on the Horizon ... 31
Chapter Four: A Strange Relationship with Death ... 40
Chapter Five: Wilmer Within ... 54
Chapter Six: The Work Begins ... 63
Chapter Seven: The End Nigh ... 80
Chapter Eight: The Unwelcome Member of the Family ... 90
Chapter Nine: the World Crumbling Once More ... 102
Chapter Ten: The Clock Starts Ticking ... 116
Chapter Eleven: Crutches ... 120
Chapter Twelve: Home ... 127
Chapter Thirteen: A Husband's Supportive Hands ... 145
Chapter Fourteen: Hyperion of Utility and Darkness ... 164
Chapter Fifteen: The Devil Closes In ... 173
Chapter Sixteen: Looking for Hope ... 187
Chapter Seventeen: The Year of Loss ... 196
Chapter Eighteen: My Own Personal Hero is Helpless ... 213
Chapter Nineteen: Into the Twilight ... 225
Authors Biography ... 240
Notes and Resources ... 246
Back Cover Material ... 275

Professor Justin Yerbury AM is a Eureka Prize-winning molecular biologist at the University of Wollongong and a world leader in motor neurone disease research. He started his scientific career after losing several family members to MND and discovering that his family carried a rare genetic form of the disease. Justin began experiencing symptoms himself in 2016 and is now ninety-nine per cent paralysed, only able to communicate using eye-gaze technology, but he continues to search for a cure. He lives in Wollongong with his wife, and his two adult daughters live close by.

For Mum and Sarah

'He who has a why to live for can bear almost any how.'

—Friedrich Nietzsche

Foreword

Jane Hawking

I much regret that I was not in Cambridge when Chris Dobson, the Master of St John's College, brought Justin Yerbury to meet my then husband, Stephen Hawking. Through Justin's account of that meeting, I now have an insight into the friendship that was established between Justin and Stephen on that occasion, but at that time had no idea of the scope of Justin's groundbreaking research, nor of his persistence in achieving it. It is thanks to this, his memoir, that I can appreciate the importance of Justin's scientific achievements, and I am honoured to be asked to write the foreword to his memoir.

Fighting Fate runs the gamut of human experience and emotion, from the carefree joy of a dedicated husband, father and sportsman to deep anxiety about Justin's family background, which led him to enrol for a degree in science. That in turn fired in him a determination to succeed in the academic arena with the result that he worked towards a PhD. The anxiety was still there, however, compounded by fear for the future. It compelled him as a postdoctoral researcher to concentrate on the science of the fatal familial version of motor neurone disease (MND), which he discovered had plagued his family for generations. Then began years of battling for grants for the survival of his group, his research into chemistry, genetics and biology – and his own income. Such is the precarious financial existence of young scientists.

By 2008 Justin's research was yielding startling results, but in the cut and thrust of life in science, his attempt to publish them was outpaced by another similar paper, from a different source, on the same subject. Deeply disappointed, Justin had to learn the hard lesson that science is as competitive – and ruthless – as any sport on the games field. Stephen learned that lesson the hard way when he presented papers about his work on black holes which contradicted the perceived wisdom of the day, but he succeeded eventually.

Justin writes clearly about his work and makes it intelligible for the untutored reader. He tells us about his research into MND, specifically on prions, misfolding proteins in the brain, which are implicated not only in the development of MND, but also Parkinson's disease and Alzheimer's. He set himself the task of searching, if not for a cure, then for a life-enhancing and life-extending treatment. He achieved encouraging results, which are nowadays used as a treatment while still undergoing greater investigation and experimentation. Justin brings his sense of humour to the fore to lighten the scientific details and comes up with astounding statistics which I will leave to the reader to discover.

Always haunted by his genetic inheritance, Justin's courage in dealing with his eventual diagnosis of MND is impressive, though his sadness is palpable. In his writing we witness his thoughts as he questioned his fate. Even so, he was determined to continue working. Not only that, he and his devoted wife, Rachel, managed to take their daughters to many of the far-flung places on their bucket list. As well I know, for a person with a disability, travelling the world indomitably is not a straightforward endeavour. What's more, only a few months ago in 2022, Justin finished writing this powerful and moving memoir. It is a biography, a scientific treatise and the personal story of a courageous fight against fate involving all his family.

Fighting Fate is a heartfelt, honest and at times heart-rending narrative that catches the reader up in the demands and tensions of a life that is being lived more fully than many others. The circumstances, of course, are some of the most extraordinarily cruel that chance can throw at anyone, and the way that Justin responds to them is very moving indeed. The fact that he is not deflected from his course and is able to follow his life's objective within science is a tribute to his intellectual, mental and emotional stamina. How he manages to sustain the energy for life in its broadest sense, and for writing this book in particular, leaves me with a sense of utmost admiration.

I hope that *Fighting Fate* will reach a wide readership. It should be compulsory reading for all members of the medical profession, especially of those who come into contact with MND patients. It will give them a much wider picture and understanding of the deeply personal aspects of the illness than they can ever deduce from a consultation.

I also wish the book every success in communicating the essence of Justin's story to all members of the public who read it. Hopefully they too will gain a clearer view of the horrors of MND and of the struggles, the fears and the anxieties that its victims and their families have to face.

Jane Hawking
Cambridge, 22 March 2023

Foreword

Bec Daniher

I was honoured to have been asked to write the foreword for this book. Justin and I have a shared passion, a shared dream. That dream is for a world without motor neurone disease.

MND is a beast. It's a progressive, terminal neurological disease that can strike anyone. People living with MND progressively lose their ability to use their limbs, speak, swallow and breathe, while their mind and senses usually remain intact. The average life expectancy is just twenty-seven months.

Justin's fight against MND began when he and his family learned that they carried a rare genetic form of the disease. Like me, he was drawn into this fight through a personal experience with the disease and has dedicated his life to the search for a cure. Justin has won national and international awards for his efforts and is one of the world's leading researchers into this terrible disease.

In a heartbreaking moment, Justin himself was diagnosed with MND in 2016. He can now only communicate with the world through his eyes. He wrote this extraordinary book that way, painstakingly typing one letter at a time with software that interprets his eye movements. All the while, the Beast continues to consume him.

As the cover of this book says, there can be no sharper lens on life than when you are faced with your own mortality.

Justin's determination, and that of his family, resonates deeply with me. It inspires and moves me to keep fighting.

Ten years ago, my family received the devastating news that my dad, Neale, had been diagnosed with MND. Like Justin, Dad had been an athlete, an AFL footballer. After some time to reflect, he responded to the news with determination. He has always told us that no matter the adversity you face, there will always be opportunity, and it's up to you to find it.

Dad's singular focus is to ensure that those who are diagnosed with MND in the future have a fighting chance to beat this beast of a disease. This can only come from an army of people who share this determination.

In 2014, FightMND was launched to shine a spotlight on MND, and to raise funds for vital research to find treatments and ultimately a cure for MND. In that time, through campaigns such as the now-famous Big Freeze, FightMND has invested $69 million into research initiatives and clinical trials, and a further $6.9 million into vital assistive equipment to help improve the lives of those living with MND. We have achieved so much, but the fight isn't over and there is still so much more to be done.

I wish more than anything that we didn't need an organisation like FightMND, but for now, we do. We joined a club we never asked to be a part of, just like Justin Yerbury. My dad and Justin are similar in many ways, not just because they have defied the odds and dedicated their lives to helping others, as you will read in this astounding book.

Justin has already done so much to fight MND, and his legacy will be immense. He has been selfless in his crusade and has brought a unique perspective to the fight, as someone who literally knows the disease inside and out. That he and his publisher, Affirm Press, are donating all of the proceeds from this book moves us at all at FightMND greatly.

Since we started FightMND, we have known that it was critical to engage as many people as possible in the battle. Like my dad, Justin can no longer speak, but the words on the pages of this book will be heard loudly throughout Australia and beyond.

THANK YOU, Justin, for being such a shining light amid so much darkness. THANK YOU, readers, for buying this book, supporting FightMND, and for recommending it far and wide so that more can join the fight to end MND.
Bec Daniher,
Campaign Director at FightMND

Author's Note

One thing that I have heavily used in my research is a microscope. It is one of the few instruments that can take you to another world. Hours and hours can be lost staring into the depths of the most mind-blowing tiny worlds. Once the specimen is prepared and has been carefully placed onto the microscope stage, I move towards the eyepiece and I notice that the light of the image flickers in and out and wobbles slightly until I am positioned perfectly. The image is like the flame of a candle, fragile and fickle. But once I have tamed it, the light is unwavering in its bright yellowish glow. Now I must focus. Turning the focus wheel towards the shadowy specimen. Unaware if I am moving the stage up or down. I focus by feel. Then it happens. The shadowy haze makes way for the crisp, clear image of the cells. A tangle of neurons wrapped in a microscopic embrace. But the microscope can never tell you the whole story. The cells have some depth to them, but at any one moment I can only see a thin slice through the cells. To know what is happening throughout the entire cell at any single moment in time is impossible. It would be like trying to know what a pig looked like by studying a slice of ham.

This book follows the same rules. It is my story, yes, but it is a thin slice of my life with many important people and events left out. This is inevitable. When focused so clearly on particular threads of my life, other moments are just right there but remain out of focus. This is my life under the microscope.

Prologue

Standing at the lectern, looking out at the audience, the grip of my anxiety tightened and tightened on my chest until it threatened to suffocate me. I hadn't felt the cold familiar fingers of fear like this in decades. The tiered seating in the lecture hall was a swollen tsunami of faces about to crash down and swallow me. In high school, my levels of anxiety had bordered on pathological, especially around public speaking.

Not now, I told myself. *Focus.*
I have worked so hard for so many years.
Trust yourself and just breathe.

The room seemed to sway under my feet, so I leaned firmly on the lectern to prop myself up. I was at Cold Spring Harbor Laboratories, in April 2016, on the private campus in Long Island, New York, which holds the most prestigious conferences in molecular biology. There were more Nobel Prize winners on this leafy campus than in all of Australia. The audience was not large, perhaps one hundred or so, although it was not the number but who they were that was important. The group of people rustling papers in expectation, waiting for me to begin my presentation, were the world's leaders in the field and now that I had their attention, I felt a strong wave of imposter syndrome flow over me.

I had grown up in a working-class neighbourhood, and I was the first in my family to go to university. I attended a school that didn't have a very academic reputation. Right now, the distance between where I had started and where I was in this moment seemed too far of a stretch, and it was creating a sinking feeling in my stomach.

But that was the least of my problems at that instant. My main concern was my thumb. It wasn't working. No matter how hard I tried, it wouldn't move. The laser pointer didn't sit right in my hand, and that scared the shit out of me. The realisation that I was dying hit me like a punch in the face, and I was reeling from it. My head was spinning. Again, I reached for the lectern to keep my balance, my whole weight now bearing down on it. Instead of seeing my life flash before my eyes, I saw my future. A paralysis creeping throughout my body, a wheelchair and a ventilator, culminating with me gasping for air, and then death. I had seen how this plays out.

Fuck.

How will I tell Rachel?

Fuck.

What about the kids?

I looked up to see the blinking eyes of the audience in anticipation. The soft murmur of impatient voices began to swell.

Okay, focus.

'I just wanted to first thank the organisers for giving me the opportunity to talk about our work. Today I would like to tell you about some of our work on amyotrophic lateral sclerosis, which is sometimes called motor neurone disease.'

Chapter One

Golden Days

I was born in Wollongong Hospital in 1974, one hundred years after the first description of the motor neurone disease la sclérose latérale amyotrophique (in English it is amyotrophic lateral sclerosis or ALS) by the French neurologist Jean-Martin Charcot, commonly known as the father of neurology. I grew up in working-class suburbia, a place where families were supported through industries such as the steelworks, oblivious that such spectacular science was happening across the globe.

After my birth, I spent the first few months of my life in and out of the children's hospital, not because any illness had befallen me but because we were there with my sister Kylie. Apparently, not only did I give my parents a distraction but I was very popular with the nurses, who loved to play with the big fat, healthy baby that came along to visit. Sadly, I have no actual memories of my sister; she died from her spina bifida when I was only three months of age. The picture I have of her in my mind is from the portrait that hung in the hall of our house at 32 Barton Street, Oak Flats. The photograph in its thin plastic frame was an important fixture of the house and the first thing that welcomed you when you entered through the front door. For most of my childhood, the pictures of Kylie, myself, and younger sisters Naomi and Sarah stood sentry over the darkened hallway. It is the one thing that we all shared. A moment in time, each at the same age, captured by the lens of a camera.

As a toddler, I could have probably been best described as active. At about ten months of age, I started to run before learning to walk. The early running start meant I didn't have enough sense to stay out of mischief. Although, as I developed and knew that I shouldn't misbehave, I still did. My mother described me as a tornado. She was a kind, loving and very maternal woman who lived vicariously through her children. She was a generous soul, and her hugs were warm, safe places. She had an understated beauty that she made little effort to expose. Her brown hair and hazel eyes foreshadowed my own features. She would painstakingly fold washed and ironed clothes into neat towering piles placed carefully on the brown and yellow tile-topped coffee table. The lounge room had a yellow and orange checked sofa, the coffee table, a TV and a stereo system that was the size of a side table. The record player often emitted the sounds of my childhood including the Beatles, Buddy Holly and the Bee Gees. Turning the AM-radio dial quickly through the stations made it talk in a strange language. As soon as Mum took her eyes off me for a second,

'Hurricane Justin' would demolish the fabric cityscape of folded washing in the blink of an eye, undoing all her efforts.

When I was four years old, I was given a gold-coloured suitcase, a Vegemite sandwich, and sent off to school. It wasn't clear that I was prepared, academically or socially, for school but what was clear was that my mother was ready for me to be busy someplace other than 32 Barton Street. If the teachers wanted proof that I was not prepared for school, they would not have to wait long. Early in that first year, I distinctly remember my kindergarten teacher making each of us stand up in front of the class and announce our street address – a task that most children did easily and proudly. I, on the other hand, was chastised in front of the class for confusing 23 for 32. I think that the teacher felt that I was getting it wrong on purpose. Across all my primary-school years I didn't have a particularly academic reputation. At the end of each school year, additional weight was added to the perpetual discussion about whether I should be kept back in that class, to redo that year. Regardless of my age and immaturity, I managed to just keep up with the other kids, so I advanced along with my classmates every year.

I can't remember being interested in science at primary school, but I definitely had a general fascination with living things as a young child. I rarely missed an episode of the Australian documentary series *The World Around Us*, and I was continually looking for lizards and other forms of life under rocks in the garden. My parents encouraged my interest in the creatures living in our garden and bought me my first microscope when I was ten. I was fascinated by the complexity of things down at the micro-level and even once tore a patch of skin off my thumb to take a closer look at my fingerprints.

From my earliest days at school, I walked the 600 metres or so from our house to the school gates, often alone. My memories of those days are cloaked in a golden glow. It makes sense to me that perhaps the glow in my memories is because those days were truly a golden period of my life. Like I am viewing these memories through gold-tinted glasses. It turns out that the golden glow in my memories is not from my warm fondness of this period but comes down to chemistry. My memories have been reinforced by photographs in our family photo album, and the photographs of the 1970s used dyes that broke down over time, leaving a golden hue across many of the photographs that has influenced and reinforced my memories. It is humbling to realise that unstable molecules have influenced the way my brain works.

My mother had also walked to school as a child, but her days were far from golden. When there was no money for shoes because her father had spent his pay cheque on beer at one of the many pubs in the town, she walked barefoot for several kilometres to get to school, and once told me that a way to warm her feet in the depths of winter was to step in fresh cow dung. In contrast, my walk to school was a safe and comfortable, well-worn path lined by now heritage-listed brush box trees. I used to know every crack in the pavement better than I knew the people in my class. I was taught that our little town had been designed by Sir Walter Burley Griffin, the architect of Australia's capital city, Canberra (so unique is the streetscape that the layout itself is now heritage listed). The town was centred on the main avenue that pointed visitors and residents alike towards the vistas of Lake Illawarra and the surrounding escarpment. The town was laid out in the 1920s, but the area was originally granted to John Horsley in 1821 and became known as the 'Oak Flats Run'. Even after the town began to take shape, the area was used as a place to run cattle.

The streets of Oak Flats that embraced the southern shore of Lake Illawarra were my backyard. While the lake has always been picturesque, it wasn't pleasant to be in, or even near, when I was young. I once walked out into the lake when I was five years old, but I turned back to shore when the pungent grey mud reached my knees. It took so long to get the stench off that I have not been in or on the waters of Lake Illawarra since. The lake has since been cleaned up by artificially opening the mouth of the lake to the Southern Pacific Ocean, meaning that seagrass no longer rots in the shallows, and the stench is all but gone. One of my first memories of walking the streets of Oak Flats is of taking twenty cents, which my parents called two bob, to the corner store so I could choose lollies one by one, which would be put into a white paper bag and twisted so none escaped. Usually, I had eaten the sweets before I got back home, so the twist was redundant. Sometimes I would be sent off down the street with much more money to get cigarettes for my dad; they were Winfield, the ones in the gold packet.

I spent day upon day walking or riding my bike around the streets. As long as I was home before the street lights came on, I had free range. It was probably in an attempt to keep those privileges that I didn't tell my parents when things were not so safe. Like the time I was racing bikes with other kids along Central Avenue. Ironically, I was riding along the footpath where I thought I would be safe from cars. I was paying too much attention to the others, and I didn't see the car reversing out of its driveway. I hit the back of the car at full speed, and tumbled over it in a complete somersault and landed on the concrete. I was not wearing a helmet because, at the time, it was not compulsory to do so. (That was not to come in to law until the late 1980s.) I was blacked out for a time, and my first memory is from the walk home on shaky legs. I did not tell my parents. In hindsight, I could have been critically injured, and no one would have known. It is a scary thought. Injuries were not always so easy to hide.

On one occasion, I gave in to the dares from the other kids, and I attempted to use a pile of gravel as a ramp. I hit the ramp at speed, and, while in the air, the bike overbalanced and I landed on the front wheel but could not regain balance. I went over the handlebars and immediately put my arms out to break my fall. I stood up and dusted myself off, and noticed the look on the other kids' faces. Something was desperately wrong. I looked down and immediately noticed my arm was just hanging there, broken. It was a complete fracture of the radius and ulna, and at that moment it looked as though I had a second elbow. The arm would need manipulation and would require a stay in hospital, which I didn't realise until I woke in a cold, dark ward in the middle of the night. I was scared and felt abandoned. I cried and then stubbornly stayed awake until my parents came back.

At the age of eleven, I walked the route to Oak Flats High School for the first time. It was a journey in the opposite direction from primary school in both a literal and metaphorical sense. I was nervous heading into my first day of high school because stories had been circulating among my fellow new students about an unofficial initiation. Word had spread that we could expect to have our heads held in a toilet while it was flushed. I had a feeling that this was going to be a very different experience from my days in primary school. By the end of that first day, I was relieved that I had escaped relatively unscathed. I had only received a punch to the stomach by the tallest kid in the school after he caught me mimicking his long, loping walk.

My initial gut feeling about the coming days of high school would prove to be true with my experience of this time having an uneasy *Lord of the Flies* flavour to it. Teenage years are supposed to be a time of personal discovery, a time when your development shapes the person you will become. But as I moved through those high-school days, I didn't really know who I was, and I didn't have a strong enough personality to find my own way. I felt like one of those cube-shaped watermelons grown in Japan. The watermelons are grown within a cube frame that restricts and controls the melon's growth, only allowing it to become the shape that is forced upon it. Just like the square watermelons of Zentsuji, I did not have the freedom to grow into the person that I would naturally have been.

I started my first year of high school in the top graded class even though I was one of the youngest in the cohort. Being young had some advantages. For example, I competed in the under-12 division for the athletics carnival. With a smaller pool of kids to participate against, I competed at the state level, only just missing out on a medal. That year I broke the school record for high-jump that still stands today, thirty-five years later.

You might imagine that being in the top class would mean that there would be limited behavioural issues but that was just not the case. The class as a group could be brutal and relentless. Once someone showed that a particular insult got under their skin the taunts grew louder and more regular. I am ashamed to say that rather than becoming an ongoing target I joined in on the game. But it was clearly not a game to those on the receiving end.

Oak Flats High School was a large campus with several sports fields and basketball courts. When I started there were over 1200 students in the school but the population was skewed to Years 7 to 10 with only a dozen or so finishing Years 11 and 12. The school was centred on two parallel double-storey buildings with the whole area smothered in concrete. It was a concrete jungle or perhaps it could be better described as a zoo. We, the students, provided the wildlife behind barred windows and the teachers spent more time controlling behaviour rather than teaching. The teachers in high school were a big change from the nurturing guidance I received in primary school.

My Year 7 maths teacher had been kicked out of the staff room because of his penchant for smoking at his desk. He was a gruff man with greying hair, large sideburns and a perpetual white piece of saliva in the corner of his mouth that could be ejected from his mouth if he yelled loudly enough. He would often yell, 'Add up the positives, add up the negatives, subtract, use the sign in front of the greater,' to teach us the basics of algebra, all the while shaking the blackboard duster up and down to the rhythm of the chant. The duster didn't leave his hand for the duration of the class except when he threw it at students not paying attention. In PE class our teacher would threaten us with various forms of torture such as hanging us from the football goal posts to throw javelins at us and would always finish his threat with ' and blood will flow'. Our history teacher always seemed like he was a living relic from the time of the ancient Egyptians that he taught us about, and was conserving his energy by speaking only a handful of words per lesson, taking long deep breaths often with his hands held in front of his face in a praying gesture. I think he often slept through class. My most reviled teacher was an English teacher, Mr H, who used humiliation as a tool to get students to do their work. He was not afraid to use anything against students, including comments about a student's weight to get them to be quiet in class. While I was among the top students in maths classes, I was perpetually at the bottom of the class in English. I found subjects that did not have clear answers, such as English, incredibly difficult. Speaking in front of the class and essay writing were particularly challenging. I never felt that I had anything of worth to write in an essay or anything to say to the class that was worth listening to. My anxiety around public speaking bordered on pathological. When I had to speak in front of the class, my stomach would churn, my knees would weaken and my voice would seemingly disappear.

In one particular essay that we were assigned, I could only muster a paragraph after being asked for two pages. In order to motivate me to do better, the teacher held my sparsely populated page up in front of the class, waving it around as if it were a flag flapping in the breeze, poking fun at it and gleefully explaining how pathetic it was. I shrank down in my chair as all heads in the room turned away from the waving page and towards me. My desire to blend in and not draw attention to myself had been found out, and I had the dreadful sense that the teacher would weaponise my anxiety and try to use it against me. However, he didn't bank on how my brain worked and would make sense of the humiliation. Instead of motivating me to write more words, he had driven me to withdraw even further than I already had. I reasoned that it was logical that if I didn't hand in any work, he could not make fun of it, so that is what I did. But, in a surprising act of defiance, I would achieve the highest marks in my class for the English exams in my final year of school.

During my early high-school years my grandfather, my father's father, died. Jack, as he was known, was a stubborn, strong man with little to say. He was bald with a long face. A face which, to my memory, changed expression very little regardless of what was happening around him. He was well known for his strength and bravery. While he was working in Captains Flat as a lift operator in an underground mine, he was in a lift accident. The lift fell into the deep water at the bottom of the mine shaft. Despite risks to his own safety he managed to drag his co-workers out of the cage from the top and to safety. When I was very young he had a stroke and much of his right side was paralysed. He later had further blood-flow issues that led to gangrenous feet that had to be amputated. This could have been avoided and easily treated if he had seen a doctor before it was too late, but his stubbornness and distrust of the medical profession meant that it went far beyond what should have been a simple treatment. Regardless of his paralysis and his missing feet he could not be kept from working on his farm. I watched as he ploughed the old granite tennis court with nothing but his wheelchair and a hoe. I like to think that I have inherited some of his dogged determination to get on with things regardless of disability. I didn't realise until after his death that his name was actually John, not Jack, and that I was given my middle name in honour of him. I am glad that I didn't know that I was named after him until I was older because I don't think that I really understood him in my earlier years. I didn't attend his funeral; I think that in some way I thought that if I didn't go it wouldn't be real.

In Year 10, there was a fracture in the group that I considered myself a part of and talking to one side meant being shunned and derided by the other side, which is what happened to me. Even after everything they put me through, for some reason I still wanted to be accepted by the group. In a way, the group fracture was the final straw. I spent my remaining lunchtimes at school on the basketball court. Basketball saved me from the barbed tongues that made high school such an uncomfortable place. It saved me from my *Lord of the Flies* deserted island. Not only was it a refuge, but it broadened my sphere, and I no longer had to rely on high-school classmates for friendship. The difference between how basketball teammates and classmates treated me was stark. I thought I had found who I was and where I was meant to be.

My first memories of basketball are going along to watch my mother and father play at the Lake Illawarra PCYC, which was called the Police Boys Club at the time. I don't remember much about the games but the squeaking of shoes on the hardwood floor and the stale smell of the sweat of dozens of people on a warm summer evening sticks in my mind. I tried my first game of basketball when I was just eleven, but I didn't know the rules so the only two times I touched the ball the referee blew the whistle for travelling and cross court penalties and gave the ball back to the other team. I didn't get back on a basketball court until the concrete courts of high school. It was on that concrete that I learned the basics and did my first slam dunk.

Basketball was a great sport for escape. While other sports like cricket or football required two or more people to practise or play, all I needed was a basketball and a hoop. It was indeed my perfect getaway. It helped that the game came naturally to me and that when I stepped onto the court, the rest of the world disappeared.

I would be selected to represent the Illawarra region in junior basketball teams. My dad was my biggest supporter. Every weekend he would take me to wherever basketball needed me to go. Dad was a relatively tall man at about six foot two but had a wingspan that must have been closer to seven feet. He had, and still has, a square face, a grey moustache, glasses and short hair meticulously parted to one side. He was a very self-confident individual, and I was always in awe of his ease and comfort in speaking to my team or any other group of people. He didn't have a formal tertiary education but was intelligent and thoughtful. In my mind, he was always a good, decent man. I wanted to be just like him. He had finished high school at fifteen and worked his way from telegram boy to a manager in head office over thirty-five years, and I respected him a lot.

I was still only sixteen years old as I entered my final year of high school, meaning that I was a full two years younger than some of the students in my grade. My young age, combined with the pressure from other students, meant that I was particularly anxious when it came to girls. My anxiety was embarrassingly crippling. I was much more comfortable being friends with the girls in my class. Other students recognised my awkwardness and would not miss an opportunity to use it against me. The same people who said I was gay for having basketball pictures on my books would taunt me for being interested in girls from our grade. While being called gay wasn't the insult they thought, the relentless nature of the taunts left me no choice but to cave in and change my book covers.

As I left high school for the very last time after finishing my final exam, I went to say thanks to my high-school basketball coach, Mr D, as he was the only teacher that I connected with at the school. I wanted to tell him what it meant to me to be a part of his team and basketball program. Before I could get those words out, he asked me what my plans for the future were. I explained that I had a plan to make the Illawarra Hawks under-21 basketball team before I turned eighteen and, after a couple of years, make the Hawks professional squad. He listened, pondered his seven years of coaching me, and said, 'Maybe you should lower your sights.' That was the last straw. My last connection with anyone at the school was burnt to the ground. The school was gone to me. It no longer existed. I walked away, vowing to have nothing more to do with the school, the teachers or my classmates ever again.

Years later, after I had started to get media attention for my science, the school invited me to come to the end-of-year presentation night to be the guest speaker. I said no. I still felt a deep revulsion for anything to do with my high school and couldn't bear the thought of going back even after twenty years. A conversation with a local surgeon who was working in the same building as me on the genetics of skin cancer, Bruce, was to turn me around. I had mentioned that I had gone to high school at Oak Flats after it had come up in conversation. I told him that they had asked me to come to their end-of-year function and give a talk. Bruce really quizzed me about my reasons for not going. He turned my reasoning on its head. He took my rationale for not going and changed it into a reason to go. He reasoned that the fact that I personally had a tough time at the school might mean that others were having an equally difficult time. Bruce looked at me across the table and said, 'Don't go back for the school. Go back to show the kids that even though you attend the poorest school in the district, you can still find success if you work hard enough.' So I called up and said that I was available to give a speech at the presentation night, after all. Ironically, I had said yes to the two things that had once made me so anxious: Oak Flats High School and public speaking. In the end I was glad I went and I realised how far I had come.

Chapter Two

A New Orbit

New Year's Eve 1991 was without a doubt the single day, from many significant days in my life, whose impact has affected the fabric of my space and time most profoundly. Its reverberations still ripple through every one of my days more than thirty years later. It changed the trajectory of my path through space, so much so that I would end up orbiting a new star. A star that shone brighter than anything I had ever known and whose warmth would light up my darkest shadows.

I had no clue what was about to happen, and I certainly wasn't looking for anything to happen that night. I was not the type of guy that went to a party looking for girls. I had been enjoying my time away from school now that I had finished my HSC exams, just hanging out and playing basketball. Mike, one of the basketball crew, was the guy who threw the now infamous New Year's Eve party. I was never a big party person, but I was much more comfortable and at ease with this group of friends than I ever was with anyone in high school, so I was actually looking forward to it. I was wearing some red and black checked pants that my mother had made for me and a black long-sleeved t-shirt.

Something that I would never have had the confidence to wear in the company of the high-school crowd. I would have been anxious, waiting for someone to make fun of them. Thinking this made me realise how comfortable in my own skin I was becoming now that I was away from that place. The only person from high school that I could handle was Sime. He was into the same basketball culture as the rest of us and couldn't care less about what you looked like or wore. He was now sporting a mohawk.

I took along with me a bottle of homemade Sambuca that my uncle Pete gave me, jumped in the car with my mates, and off we went. There were quite a few people at the party, many of whom I did not know. I guessed that most of these were from Mike's high school. Early on in the evening, we bundled into the car to go pick up some more alcohol. It was a small car, old, but in good condition. We fit six people in the car, four squashed across the back leather seats. As we unfolded ourselves from the vehicle, someone noticed that I was wearing a Chicago Bulls cap backwards and suggested it made me look younger, which could foil our plan to look old enough to buy alcohol, given we were all under eighteen still. I went back to the car and gave my hat for safekeeping to one of the girls still sitting in the car. The girl's name was Rachel. Rachel had a cute heart-shaped face, long blonde hair and a personality many times bigger than her small frame. She was wearing a white crocheted top that was more hole than top, maroon jeans and matching maroon Doc Martens boots. My previous anxiety around girls was melted away by Rachel's warmth that night. It felt just right. She was beautiful, funny and confident. I was hooked.

I had planned to be picked up from the party by my parents after midnight, but Rachel asked me to stay. I called my mum to ask if that would be okay, and Rachel said, 'Why are you asking? You've finished school so can make up your own mind.' I felt a pang of anxiety. I knew that I didn't belong and that I had been found out for the naïve and socially challenged person that I was. In the end, I did stay, and I slept alongside Rachel on the floor of Mike's living room with a dozen or so other people. I tentatively put my arm around her as we drifted off to sleep.

While I had asked her to hold only my hat, Rachel had taken – stolen – my heart when I had my guard down. I needed to see her again so I asked for her phone number. I didn't wait long to call her; it was only the next day, but I couldn't wait any longer. When I called and asked for Rachel and the voice on the phone said she wasn't home, I thought that I was being rejected. I asked, 'Are you sure she's not there,' and the voice repeated that she was out. The more I spoke, the more I was convinced that I was talking to Rachel on the phone and she didn't want to see me. It made sense to me that she would not want to see me again, given my view of myself. So I hung up, resigned to the fact that I would never see her again. It turned out that it was her younger brother Damien on the phone, and she was at a funeral. I had never been happier about someone attending a funeral.

That summer I felt that the shackles of my old life had been removed, that I was free from judging eyes. I was the most free that I had ever been, or at least it felt like that. It was wonderful not to have to worry that anything that I said or did would be scrutinised and made fun of. There seemed to be a party every other night that summer, and if I wasn't working out on the basketball court, I was hanging out with Rachel. I had fallen deeply in love. I didn't know it was possible. We were inseparable, we went everywhere together, and we talked for hours every night. Rachel even took me to the special place she would go to for peace and solitude on the cliffs of the Minnamurra Headland. We shared our secrets and dreams in that intense first summer. I felt completely accepted for the first time in my life.

On the one occasion that Rachel couldn't stay at one of the many parties we went to, I phoned her once she was home. It wasn't the same without her. She said that she couldn't come back because she was looking after her brothers. I asked her to sneak out, but she wouldn't. I called her back to serenade her by singing along to Gang Starr's 'Lovesick' but I only made it to the line where the girl hangs up the phone because that's exactly what Rachel jokingly did. I was definitely lovesick.

I didn't want that summer to end. Many years later a song by Josh Pyke would bring back the memories of that summer: 'We should be living like we lived that summer...' They came flooding back. The memories make me happy but also there is a little sadness that comes along with them. That summer was a symbol of the carefree days before our world started falling apart. I now have my very own version of 'The Summer' that Josh Pyke recorded for me. There is no way that he could ever fully understand what his song means to me.

The summer would eventually come to an end. Rachel went back to high school, where she was now in Year 12, and I started my commerce degree at the University of Wollongong. I had been awarded a position in the course because of my scores in the trial HSC. I topped my grade with that very unexpectedly high mark in English. The guaranteed place at the university reduced my motivation to study for the final exams, and my final tertiary entrance ranking was seventy, meaning that I was in the top thirty per cent of students that took the HSC that year. That was a very average mark. It certainly was not anything that would suggest an academic career.

Rachel's parents didn't want her to be distracted for her final year of high school, so they told her it would be better not to see me much if at all. They thought that Rachel had to choose between good grades and me. Despite their warnings, we saw each other most days that year. Even with Rachel spending most of her time studying, we would still sit together and just hang out. I hadn't yet learnt to drive so I caught the train to Minnamurra from Oak Flats many times. At the time there was rarely anyone at the stations so I rode for free most of the time. The trains between Oak Flats and Minnamurra were diesel trains commonly referred to as red rattlers. The old trains had doors and windows that could be opened; this was the time before automatic doors. On many an evening I would stand in the doorway and holding on with one hand let myself swing outside the door as the train rounded a corner. Feeling the breeze rushing around me with the train moving at speed through the evening air, I felt so free.

Rachel was very much welcomed into our family. My mother, in particular, loved her very much. Although, at times, Rachel found my mother's interest in what we were doing a little smothering. I didn't really notice, having grown up with it. One could have said that Rachel and I were smothering each other with the amount of time we spent together, but it never felt like that. I would even go along with Rachel to her evening art sessions at her school. On one occasion, I climbed part the way up the mezzanine ladder in the art room, leaned over as far as I could, and wrote J♡Rach in chalk on the brick wall. I thought that it would be high enough and far enough away from the mezzanine that it might stay for a few weeks, and Rachel might see it in class. Years later, when we visited the school with our daughter Talia for an open day, it was still there. It remained as a symbol of our enduring love even though, by some people's early accounts, our bond was as frail as chalk on a wall. At the end of Rachel's final year of school, in a moment that perhaps foreshadowed her tenacity and her never-give-up attitude when it comes to me, Rachel was told that I couldn't attend her graduation ceremony as it was just students and family, and even after further requests being flat out refused, she took me anyway.

Rachel would finish her high-school studies in October 1992, and her parents' fears did not come to pass. Despite spending a lot of time with me, she got incredibly high grades, finishing within the top five per cent in the state. The takeaway message was beware of telling Rachel she can't do something. Rachel was extremely bright, strong, and a very confident individual, which was in stark contrast to me at the time. I had little motivation, and little confidence in social situations. I was racked with anxiety such that I had trouble even talking to sales staff in stores. Case in point, I bought a heart-shaped locket for Rachel's eighteenth birthday, but I couldn't force myself to talk to the engraver. After working myself into a tightly wound ball of anxiety, I was unable to do anything, so I asked Rachel to go in and do it. Yes, I asked her to help with her own present. In the end, because of my anxiety, there was a mistake in the engraving, and instead of the date of her eighteenth birthday, Rachel's date of birth was engraved on the locket. Although she still loved me regardless of my many broken and imperfect parts, it was clear then that something had to change. It was Rachel who taught me how to cope in the world and held my hand while I gradually began to increase my interaction with people in all kinds of social settings. Eventually, I would give lectures to hundreds of people and meet international scientists for my work. Without Rachel's love and support, none of that would have been possible.

Early in our relationship we developed a love for the rainforest at Macquarie Pass National Park on the Illawarra escarpment. I had always loved the outdoors and enjoyed camping but a particular place had never held such a special place in my heart before this. We went several times with friends and also started going to the Clover Hill Road section ourselves. I think part of the attraction was that there were no trails and no camping grounds but just spectacular waterfalls and beautiful rainforest blanketed in a soft green coat of moss and ferns. It felt like one of the last wild places that was available to us. It had a beauty that I could only see through the lens of Rachel. She brought beauty into my life and taught me to appreciate nature.

On one trip we made to the rainforest we tried a new way of walking downriver to avoid some of the huge canyons. We had gone a decent distance down the steep ravine when Rachel twisted her ankle on a rock. There was no way that she could walk and climb out of there, so I carried her up. It made me feel valued to know that while Rachel could psychologically carry me out of a dark place, at least I could physically carry her when she needed me. Macquarie Pass would continue to hold a special place in our hearts and we would get photos there for our wedding and would go on to make a tradition of our pilgrimage to the rainforest for our wedding anniversary.

My after-school plan that my high-school basketball coach had unceremoniously shot down had begun to take shape. I had successfully made the youth team. The team had players that were in the Hawks professional squad, and, as I was one of the younger players, I learned a lot from those guys. I got another step closer to my goal by training with the Hawks squad and playing with the bench players in the men's Sydney competition, which we also won that same year.

After such a successful year, I signed a contract with the Hawks for the 1995 season. I had put the work in, and just three years after being told that I should lower my sights, I had achieved exactly what I had set out to. In the National Basketball League, I had the opportunity to travel to cities around the country. It was the first-ever time that I had been on a plane, and the first time I had been out of New South Wales since a trip my family had taken to Western Australia when I was four. Every aspect of professional sports seemed glamorous to me and the sound of thousands of people cheering me on after I'd hit a long three-point basket or chased down an opponent and blocked their shot into the backboard flowed through my body and spurred me on. It was like nothing that I had experienced before. My claim to fame was the block that I just mentioned made it to the plays of the week on Channel Ten's basketball show.

On the basketball court, I was a different person. I was driven, committed and passionate. And talking wasn't an issue. Getting into an opponent's mind was fair game if you could back it up with how you played. I wished that some of that grandiose self-confidence could have spilled over into the rest of my life, but for the time being it remained squarely inside the painted lines of the basketball court.

I had been passing all my subjects at university while I was working away at my basketball. I had been thinking that marketing could be a good career. Interning at the Hawks in sports marketing would have been ideal, but I didn't have the confidence to ask if that would be possible. At the time, the popularity of basketball was increasing, and sports marketing was a huge deal globally. But in contrast to those lofty ambitions, my grades were average at best and could be summed up by a few quotes from a friend, Mat D, who would say Ps[1] get degrees, and if you get fifty-one per cent, that means that you've put in one per cent too much effort.

Rachel and I continued to spend every day together. We did everything together. We took road trips in our little green Ford Laser. We studied, slept and lived together. It just felt right. I don't know how you know that someone is the right one for you, but if it doesn't feel right when they aren't there with you, then that is probably a sign. We knew pretty early that we had something special, and I knew that I would spend the rest of my life with her. We could talk all night and still have something to say in the morning. I knew that Rachel would be there for me whenever I needed her and that with her holding my hand walking alongside me, I could do anything.

I never got down on one knee or took Rachel to a fancy restaurant to propose to her. We had always talked about it, and eventually it just happened. We announced our engagement together like we did everything together. We were not going to follow any traditions just because that was how things were supposed to

---

[1] Ps stands for a Pass grade.

be done. As long as we were together. We moved into a little one-bedroom flat before we got married so that we could have our own space. We organised to get married by the mouth of the Minnamurra River. In the language of the traditional owners, Minnamurra means plenty of fish. It must have been a nurturing haven for the original Australians for tens of thousands of years. I, too, had found my nurturing haven, but it was not a place. With Rachel, I had that everywhere I went.

I was on top of the world. I was about to marry my best friend and although being a professional basketball player only paid five thousand dollars per year I thought that I had the best job in the world.

Our wedding day in February 1995 started out cloudy and grey, but when it was time to say 'I do', the clouds parted, and the sun shone down on our little ceremony.

My uncle, my mother's brother Ken, had his arm in a sling at our wedding. Ken, or Kenny as he was always known, was a charismatic man with a friendly face and balding head. One of my fondest memories of Kenny is a debate that we had when I was about ten about which Harrison Ford character was the best, Han Solo or Indiana Jones. I was on the Star Wars side of the argument, but he was very convincing. He was much loved by the family.

Kenny had noticed something wasn't quite right with his shoulder while playing golf. It was months later in the September of 1994 that he was diagnosed with some mysterious condition called motor neurone disease. Three letters that tore lives apart, MND. Kenny had the ALS form of the disease. It was a disease that no one I knew had heard of, let alone experienced. Initially, we didn't really understand what the diagnosis meant for Kenny, and we certainly didn't know what it meant for our family as a whole.

Chapter Three

Storm Clouds on the Horizon

Paris, late 1870s. Jean-Martin Charcot was standing quietly at the front of the stately, high-ceilinged lecture theatre in the Pitié-Salpêtrière Hospital, holding the attention of the students and junior doctors wearing black three-piece suits and bow ties in the tiered rows of seats. A stout man with a barrel chest and his hair swept back, Charcot commanded the utmost respect, there in his element, like a Roman emperor. With one exception – a nurse – there were no women in this scene, just serious men taking themselves very seriously.

Every Tuesday, Charcot performed demonstrations for his students and visitors. He would have a patient brought into the small lecture theatre, a room overlooking the gardens outside through its large, gold-curtained windows, the steeples of the churches of Paris visible in the distance. Occasionally the patients were presented to Charcot before he had seen them so that he could diagnose them for the audience.

Today's demonstration included a patient with MND. After the examination, he leaned in and said something quietly to the patient, comforting him. Charcot's voice was soft so the students could not hear what he said. He then asked the nurse to take the man back to the ward. He turned to the audience as he waited for the patient to be taken out of the room. Once again, he had the full attention of the room, and he said, 'Now that the patient is no longer here, we can and must speak amongst ourselves in total frankness. The most varied remedies with the most logical bases will be entirely impotent to slow the progressive advance of this disease. It is sad to say, but it is true.'

His apparent tenderness and sympathy for his patient at that moment belied his reputation. Charcot could be a cold, quiet, difficult and authoritarian figure. So much so that he was often referred to as Napoleonic, but his apparent power and his intense devotion to his students earned him a disciple-like following.

He continued. 'However, for the doctor, whether it is sad or not is not the issue: truth is the issue. Let us keep looking in spite of everything. Let us keep searching, for it is indeed the best method for finding. And perhaps, thanks to our efforts, the verdict we will give such a patient tomorrow will not be the same as we must give him today.'

It was during this moment that the seeds of MND research were planted. Charcot, with elegant clarity, had identified the significance and indeed necessity of MND research that rings true even in the present day. MND is still an untreatable, incurable and fatal disease. Before we can treat it, we must understand it.

It was 1874 when Jean-Martin Charcot first characterised the motor neuron tracts in the spinal cord after he analysed the nervous system of a patient who died of a creeping paralysis. He called the condition la sclérose latérale amyotrophique. In English, it is amyotrophic lateral sclerosis (ALS), which, when translated into everyday language, means muscular wasting (atrophy) with scarring in the lateral tract of the spinal cord. It is an apt description of the condition and a definition that persists to the present day.

ALS is the most common of the motor neurone diseases. In fact, it makes up such a large proportion of these disorders that in some countries it is simply referred to as motor neurone disease (MND), as is the case in Australia and the UK. It is invariably fatal, usually between two and five years after diagnosis, although there are rare exceptional cases where people survive for decades, as was the case for Stephen Hawking. Around eighty per cent of people diagnosed with the motor neurone disease ALS do not survive past five years after being diagnosed. Death typically results from respiratory failure and, more rarely, inanition (essentially starvation) or falls.

Motor neurons are the nerve cells that connect the brain to the voluntary muscles in every part of the body. There are two main types, the first in the brain and the second in the spinal cord. They have laid down extremely long axons (nerve fibres) like train tracks so that the neurons that start in the brain connect to those in the spinal cord which in turn have long tracks to the muscle. When you think about moving your arm, the signal boards a train in the brain, travels to the spinal cord, changes train, and then travels out to the muscles.

I have become increasingly aware over the last two decades that the brain is an amazing thing and that the motor neurons that reside there are a particularly vulnerable minority. While there are an estimated one hundred billion neurons in the brain, the number of motor neurons is more in the order of hundreds of thousands. A drop in the ocean of brain cells. Let me put it this way: if the London Underground moving five million people per day was equivalent to the brain, a single line carrying only ten passengers would represent all the motor neurons in the nervous system. If one of the trains in Underground lines in London was out of service, while it would be annoying, most of the five million passengers would get to their destination. On the other hand, if our hypothetical motor neuron train went down, one hundred per cent of the system would be affected. The motor system is so vulnerable that it is astonishing that things do not go wrong more often. Given the dependence of every movement we make on the precise performance of the brain, when things do go wrong, it can be absolutely devastating.

Within months of my uncle Ken noticing something was wrong with his shoulder, his arm was totally paralysed. Our wedding would be the last time my mother and her siblings would all be together in one room. We had no idea how fast things would unravel. I would never see Ken again after our wedding weekend. He went downhill very fast and did not survive the year. In fact, he would only live another six months after our wedding. He died in August 1995.

Having watched Ken's rapid demise up close and personal, his wife was concerned that perhaps this awful thing could be inherited and passed down to their daughter. So, the question was put to their doctor in Canberra, who in turn asked a colleague in Sydney, Dr Roger Pamphlett, whose interest lay in the genetics of neurological disease. Dr Pamphlett confirmed that the condition could be inherited in some cases but wanted to make it absolutely clear to them that this was rare. Instead, most cases of MND are sporadic or seemingly random throughout the population.

There had been anecdotal evidence that some cases of MND clustered in families as far back as Charcot's first description of the disease in the nineteenth century. One of the earliest reports of the possibility of inheritance was by Dr G. Wilse Robinson from Kansas City in 1917. However, with the incomplete understanding of genetics at the time, it was impossible to say for certain whether family clusters like this were inherited or caused by an environmental factor that the entire family group was exposed to. As we understand it today, genetic inheritance was first discovered by the Augustinian monk and biologist Gregor Mendel in the mid-nineteenth century. He published his work from over a decade of observations in 1865. Mendel studied clear-cut and easy-to-identify traits such as seed colour in peas. His work was rediscovered in the early part of the twentieth century by a small number of researchers. Still, it would be decades before the science would be broadly recognised, understood and appreciated.

In stark contrast to the distinct traits Mendel worked with, identifying MND was not as clear-cut at the time. Even fifty years after Charcot's description of ALS, there was little consensus on what to call the creeping paralysis, and it was often recorded under several names on death certificates. Each case of MND is unique, presenting with a distinct pattern of symptoms and variable age of onset. Further complicating the identification of inheritance is the fact that some genetically predisposed people may die from other causes before developing MND. In the early twentieth century this was not uncommon, because while the average age of onset of MND is between the ages of forty-five and sixty-five, the average life expectancy in the Western world in 1900 was forty years of age. This means that even if Mendel's rules were applied in those early stages of MND research, the arrangements of cases within a family would likely not have been recognised as a pattern of inheritance anyway. Even into the 1920s and '30s, the general consensus among neurologists was that MND wasn't familial or inherited, regardless of the smattering of papers published that claimed that it was. It wasn't until Leonard T. Kurland and Donald W. Mulder collated the literature and several case studies in 1955 that it became crystal clear that MND could be passed on from one generation to the next. Kurland and Mulder concluded from the evidence on hand that the disease was dominantly inherited in around nine per cent of cases.

In the late 1980s, the technology had evolved such that it was possible to start narrowing down where in the genome the genetic defects that cause the inherited form of MND might lie. Dr Teepu Siddique from Northwestern University, Chicago, found that a region of chromosome 21 contained the inherited congenital defect responsible for MND in some American families. Arising from that initial genetic discovery, Dr Robert 'Bob' Brown and Daniel Rosen made a breakthrough discovery in 1993. They reported that the defects found in chromosome 21 were in a gene called SOD1. The SOD1 gene codes, or provides instructions, for the protein called Cu/Zn superoxide dismutase.

The function of the Cu/Zn superoxide dismutase enzyme is to convert reactive superoxide molecules into less dangerous products. Superoxide molecules are a by-product of producing energy that can damage DNA and other cellular structures. This role of the Cu/Zn superoxide dismutase enzyme is so vital that without it, lifespan is significantly reduced. Given what was known about the activity of the enzyme at the time, it was logical for researchers to immediately think that the reason mutations in SOD1 caused MND was that they disrupted the enzyme's important cellular antioxidant function. But that was not the end of the story. In fact, it was only the beginning.

In 1994 Teepu Siddique and Mark Gurney published a paper describing the genetic engineering of a mouse that would act as a model of ALS for decades to come. The mice were generated by inserting the mutated human form of SOD1 into their DNA. The mice developed a motor neurone disease and did not survive past five to six months of age, which is a drastic reduction down to twenty-five per cent of a lab mouse's average life span. Tellingly, the mouse retained functional enzyme activity, demonstrating that the toxic effects of the mutations were not simply due to a loss of SOD1 activity. Instead, the mutated form must have gained a new function that made it toxic.

Since that first genetic discovery, there are now dozens of genes in which mutations are known to cause MND. There are also many more genetic mutations that are thought to be risk factors. Which is to say that carrying certain genetic changes may give a person a higher than normal chance of getting the disease. So, there is currently a school of thought that says all cases of MND have some genetic aspects, which is a total reversal of thought from a century ago.

Luckily for our extended family, Dr Pamphlett had assured us in his letter that the inherited form is rare. So any fleeting thoughts of inheritance after Uncle Ken's diagnosis and subsequent death were quickly quashed.

Chapter Four

A Strange Relationship with Death

It was mid-1996. I sat opposite my cousin Ashley at my small dining-room table. I had trouble meeting his eyes, and my gaze drifted to the glass tabletop where his image was reflected, like his whole world, upside down. I hadn't heard much of what he had said. His voice had wavered and was a scratchy version of its previous smooth tones, but that is not why I didn't hear him. Ashley had come to tell me that he was dying, that he had MND. I heard very little after these words. I had been told this tragic news before this visit by my aunt, but it hadn't made this any easier. Ashley was twenty-one years old. Still a kid.

My gaze drifted back to Ashley but didn't dwell long before it wandered to the ceiling to rest on the repeating patterns of the decorative cornices of the half-house that Rachel and I were renting. *What is MND?* I thought. *How does a person die from it?* It had been just over a year since Kenny had died, but I had never thought to ask how. I wondered if Ashley knew more about what was in store for him, but I was too scared to ask. I had read that MND strikes people in their forties or fifties, so it seemed like a cruel nightmare that Ashley had been given this death sentence at such a young age.

He had always been thin, perhaps wiry is a better word, but as he sat across from me, labouring for every breath, he was thinner than usual. Despite everything, he still managed a smile. Ashley had always been the archetypal little brother, which had given him a chip on his shoulder. Regardless of his small frame, he never backed down from a fight, no matter the odds. He would rather go into a fight knowing that he would lose than back down to anyone. But I got a sense, as I sat across from him, that he had lost the fighting spirit and that this foe was too big even for him. Ash had a long, freckled face with a contagious smile so constant that it might have been stuck that way when the wind changed – as our parents used to warn us would happen. In contrast to his older brother, Jamie, he had a light complexion, and his mop of blond hair was thinning even at his young age. Ashley was my first cousin, my mother's sister Kathy's second son. I had grown up with Ashley and Jamie as a key part of my extended family. They had lived with our grandparents on Telegraph Road in Young throughout their entire teenage years, and we would always hang out whenever we visited my grandparents, which was most summers.

Family was always a big part of our lives, and my mother always kept in very close contact with her brothers and sisters. Two of Mum's sisters and their families moved close to our house in Oak Flats, and so for many years we saw my mother's family every weekend. My mother was the eldest of eight children, with five sisters and two brothers. How they all fit into the house on Telegraph Road growing up, I don't know. But somehow, they came out as adults that were still very close. Exploring the farms and paddocks of Young with Jamie and Ashley had given me a sense of independence as a kid. There were no questions asked about where we were going or when we would be home. We were a brotherhood. Bound together by feats of bravery and protecting one another. Together we walked across the rickety wooden train bridge, never knowing if a train was going to come. At different times Ashley had stopped me from being bitten by a brown snake and from being attacked by bees when I tried to get honeycomb from the hollow of a tree. We shared a strong bond just as we shared the adventures of exploration of the creeks, hills and old rundown buildings. So many good memories. They will stay with me forever.

Although we used to spend day after day together in Young, at the moment that he told me he was dying, I hadn't known what to say to Ashley. I had no experience talking to someone who was dying. I had no reference point. Nothing I could anchor my conversation on. Because of the early death of my older sister, death had been a taboo subject all my life, and I carried that with me still. Even while death sat across from me and slapped me in the face, I still could not acknowledge it. I realised that this was a selfish way of approaching the situation, but I could not bring myself to talk about it. Any questions or words of comfort were caught up in the tight ball in my chest. I should have asked Ash how he really was. I should have asked what he thought about death, and I should have told him I loved him. But I didn't.

Even today, I am unsure what frightened me the most about Ashley's diagnosis. I didn't know enough about MND, so I didn't know if he would be in pain or how the disease would end up killing him, and that scared me. The unknown, so many unknowns, made me feel uneasy. I struggled with the concept of death. An infinite amount of time of nothingness seemed the likely result of death and I found thoughts of infinity and death extremely unsettling. I had always felt that death was something not to be talked about.

Even as a child when I wanted to know about death and what happened to my sister Kylie, I was too afraid to ask. I didn't want to make my parents have to think about the loss of their child. Life seemed extremely fragile and such a statistical anomaly against the backdrop of the vast lifeless universe. I tried to keep these thoughts away from the front of my mind because too much thinking about it could interfere with and bog down the inner workings of my mind.

I grew up with a strange relationship with death. My sister Kylie had died before my first memories, and my parents never spoke about her. I felt that I couldn't ask about Kylie or death. As a result, death was mysterious to me. I thought perhaps I could get some answers about death from school since we had a scripture class once a month. I was young, so I was naïve as to how the classes might be able to help me. There were no answers about death itself, only stories about how to get to the magical place called heaven. They told me that if I didn't go to church, I would probably go to hell. I asked about Kylie. She was only a baby. Surely she would have gone to heaven. The teacher said no, she would have been judged by my parents' actions and was likely to have gone to hell. I closed all doors to religion at that moment. I didn't think it made any sense. Even at the age of five, I thought it smelled like the cow dung Mum had stepped in to warm her feet.

The subject of death was so taboo in my family that my pet animals never died, they just 'ran away'. I only discovered this secret and its cover-up after I had my own kids. In hindsight, my parents missed an opportunity to teach us about grief and death with our pets, and I think that I suffered later in life because of it. I remember that the only person who died during that period of my life was my uncle, my father's sister Kay's husband. He had cancer. I was young and didn't know him very well, and so I didn't process it, and I didn't deal with it. There wasn't even any question that we would go to the funeral. Our parents dropped us at a friend's house and left us to think about his death on our own. Around the same time, I realised that once I died there would be an eternity of nothing. In my mind, it equated to an infinite sense of falling in a dream without ever waking up. It made a hole in my stomach just thinking about it. What was the point of living a relatively short life if we would spend eternity in some kind of limbo? Without any guidance on how to feel about death and how to cope with my feelings about it, the existential angst lasted for weeks after my conversation with Ashley.

I couldn't quite bring myself to believe that Ashley was really dying. I found myself thinking, *Are we sure that this disease that Ashley has is the same thing that Kenny had? Maybe they got it wrong.* Kenny started with symptoms in his shoulder while Ashley first had symptoms in his throat. He lost his voice on a fishing trip, so it seemed altogether different. For many months he thought that it was a typical, albeit stubborn, sore throat. He saw doctor after doctor, but nothing helped. It was only when my aunt Gay felt that it could be MND that Ashley went to see the neurologist. I am not sure how she picked it up, but I suspect she saw something in Ashley that she had seen in Kenny. I wanted to ask how long the doctor said he would live, but I didn't. I knew that the doctors told him that there was nothing to be done and that he should get his affairs in order. I just couldn't bring myself to talk to him about it. Instead, I chose to ignore the space that MND was occupying between us and I resolved to regale him with a tale from my so far short professional basketball career.

I painted the picture of how sitting in the locker room with the seasoned professional athletes in itself was a great feeling. The locker room was always a hive of activity with physiotherapists providing treatment for some players, and the smell of Dencorub mixed with medical tape and sweat filling the room. Some of the guys sat with ice on their legs. Others elevated their legs on chairs. I told Ashley how one particular day it had been a good practice session, and at some points it got heated. The locker room always became a debrief session as well as a space for the cooldown of aching bodies after practice. Questions were asked of players if it was thought they didn't work hard enough or if the play got too physical. There was also just general banter and trash talk between a bunch of competitive guys. Sometimes it would go too far. On this particular day the guys were letting one of the players know that he hadn't worked hard enough. Eventually he lost his cool and shouted, 'That's it, fuck all of ya, I'm going to my car to get my gun.' We didn't know if he was serious or if he had a gun at all, but we didn't hang around to find out. After all, he had served time in prison. We scrambled over one another to get out of the locker room and escaped out the back door of the stadium.

As I had been telling Ash the story, Rachel prepared some sandwiches. This simple act would show us MND up close and personal for the first time. While I speedily devoured the sandwiches on my plate, we noticed that Ashley had only managed one or two bites. As I watched more carefully, I could see that Ashley struggled to swallow even a single bite. For a brief moment, I prepared myself to get up and clear his blocked throat. I apologised profusely for not realising that eating the sandwich would be a problem and said, 'I'll get you something else,' but he politely declined. It was clear that this hideous disease was not likely to end in an easy death.

Ashley asked about our daughter, Talia, who was sleeping in the next room.

Months after Rachel and I were married, we had found out we were pregnant. We were only twenty-one, and this was not a part of the immediate plan. After the initial shock, we settled into the idea of becoming parents. At the time, we were still kids finding our place in the world. At least in my mind, we grew up quickly and immediately. On my first day as a father in January 1996, I found my dad voice when a kid ran past where I was holding a newborn Talia in the hospital corridor. 'Slow down,' I bleated, at which the kid stopped and started to walk.

In truth, Rachel and I didn't know how we would cope. Parenthood was harder than we could have ever imagined. Talia didn't sleep well, and it seemed to be getting harder and harder, not easier. Rachel carried most of the burden as most of the waking at night could be comforted by breastfeeding. At the time, we thought our lives were particularly challenging. We had no idea what tough really was.

We were by no means well off financially. I worked at Figtree post office in the morning, then trained with the Hawks during the day and then with West Sydney during the evening. Rachel also worked part time as a youth worker, while pursuing her psychology registration, so we got by. I loved being a dad and loved my time with Talia. I was able to spend time with my daughter because I didn't work regular hours while Rachel worked as a youth health worker. Sometimes I would even take Talia in to Rachel for a breastfeed in her break or take her to basketball training and put the pram at the side of the court.

Although I loved being a dad, I didn't always make the right decisions. One day I had Talia in a baby carrier as we were heading out to the back yard to put the clothes on the washing line. I put her on the bed in the back room for a few moments and carried the washing basket out to the line. I went back to get Talia only to find that the door had closed behind me and locked me out. I ran around the house looking for an unlocked door or window so I could get back inside to my baby daughter. Nothing. I sprinted back to the back window, and could see Talia getting upset. I had no choice but to smash a window. For some reason that I cannot explain I decided to break the window closest to Talia. So, after I broke it there was glass all around her. I chalked that one up as a learning moment. We learned more and more each day.

One thing raising a little baby girl did was to provide a distraction from the last few months of Ashley's life. I didn't want to face the reality of Ashley's impending death. I also didn't want to admit to myself what the implications for our family were of Kenny and Ashley both having MND.

I found myself feeling so helpless talking to Ashley once he had been diagnosed. I wanted to be able to say that doctors knew what caused MND and that there was a treatment on the horizon. But I couldn't say anything. I didn't know anything and didn't understand the things I read on the internet when I tried to find answers. Initially, I couldn't tell useful information from the misinformation that was on the internet. There was some persuasive information that I read claiming that MND was caused by vaccines because at the time there was a real cluster of returning soldiers from the Gulf War with MND. Of course, one thing in common all of these soldiers got before deployment was vaccinations. But the more you read and dug into a story like that, the more you discovered that it was not based on any hard evidence.

I don't know what made me think that I would be able to understand it. I just knew that the doctors had told Ashley to go home and get his affairs in order, and I felt that it was not good enough and that someone should be doing something proactive. Why would they just leave him to fend for himself like this?

A few months later, I received a phone call. Ashley was dead. He had died overnight. He was in his bed at Nan and Pop's place. Alone.

Even though we knew that this was coming, it was still a shock. 'What happened?' I asked. 'I thought he was doing okay.'

Ashley had been having trouble sleeping because of the twitching. The fasciculations – involuntary muscle contractions and relaxations. A symptom of MND that the entire family would all be haunted by from this point onwards.

A doctor had prescribed a muscle relaxant, hoping to suppress the twitching and let him sleep. Perhaps that had contributed to his death. How much had he taken? All these thoughts were distractions from the questions that I should have been asking.

How was he feeling?

Why wasn't someone there with him?

Why wasn't I there?

How was everyone up there in Young?

Rachel and I were in our little green car on the way to the funeral. The fields of parched yellow grass, the gum trees, and the curves in the road seemed to speed towards us as we sat motionless in the car. A rainbow appeared on the horizon in what felt like a symbol of hope. We snapped a photo as the world moved beneath the wheels of the car. It became my enduring memory of this day.

At the church, everything was a haze. People were speaking, but I didn't hear what they were saying. I felt stationary and numb as people moved in a blur around me. Tears flowed as I helped carry the coffin out of the church. I felt the weight of his body for the last time. He was here on this earth – the heaviness of his body confirmed it – and I sensed his loss deeply as we placed him gently in the hearse. I searched for Jamie, my cousin, Ashley's older brother. His name was synonymous with Ashley and rarely spoken individually. Jamie and Ashley. Like Batman and Robin or Ernie and Bert. Now without his little brother, I held Jamie as activity swirled around us. I said nothing, but I hoped he understood what it was that I wasn't saying.

I have never really been very good at identifying my emotions. At least not in any meaningful way. I was upset, sad, scared, angry and confused. My body was a clenched fist, and I needed to hit something. Or run or scream. I didn't really know. I had a strange feeling of fear that was hard to describe. I couldn't say what it was that I was afraid of, and I think that was the crux of my uneasiness. I recalled I had felt this feeling in another context. On the escarpment, several kilometres from our house, overlooking the lake and ocean, alongside the train line was a tunnel that was started but never finished. It must have been a hundred metres or so into the hillside. It had been gated off, but someone had created a hole big enough to clamber through. As I had walked into the tunnel, the sunlight faded more and more until eventually the light came to a point where it almost disappeared over what seemed like a bed. As I'd stood there taking in the scene, I realised that someone had been sleeping there, perhaps living there. Then it hit me: what if the person living there was actually *still* in there? Right now. I couldn't see anything that was in the shadows. The darkness was absolute. If I extended my arm out in front of me, it was lost in the inky blackness. I felt the acute uneasiness of being vulnerable because I did not know what was in the darkness. Was there someone right in front of me about to strike me with a stone or a knife? My heart started pounding so hard it threatened to escape my chest. I turned back towards the light, and before my eyes even adjusted to the brightness, I left. Sadly, there was no walking away from MND.

Even weeks after we lost Ashley, I was still angry at the medical profession for not providing any light in the dark corners of MND. Not only was there no cure, no understanding of what caused MND, they had also left Ashley alone through this horrendous process.

The pain of Ashley's death continued to sting and it wasn't subsiding. I had to put my pain under the microscope before I realised that the very thing that made my blood boil about the medical profession was the very same thing that I had done. I had to admit to myself that I had also abandoned Ashley. I didn't manage to find time to visit Ashley, and calling wasn't viable given the effects of MND on his voice. I didn't support Ashley through those days, through the most challenging part of his life. I felt like such a fucking arsehole. Not only a fucking arsehole but also a coward. It is clear to me now that this abandonment at least partly explains the visceral reaction that I had to Ashley's death. I let him go through it on his own. I deeply regret now the priority that I gave to basketball at that stage of my life. I should have spent more time with Ashley, and also, at the same time, I should have been there more often for Rachel. I think that basketball, which I once saw as a saving grace, had become a distraction from the realities of my life.

While this immense feeling of guilt may not have been the factor that sustained my drive and dedication to shining a light on the dark corners of MND, it was undoubtedly the match and can of petrol that started the fire.

Chapter Five

Winter Within

My muscles were a ball of tension. I was a spring wound tightly. I needed to somehow release the enormous tension that had coiled up inside me. I vowed to use the nervous energy I felt to get some answers. To take a light and shine it on the shadows that haunted my family. I decided then that if no one else could tell me what was happening, I would have to find out myself. The first thing that I wanted to know was about the inheritance of MND. If this MND was truly inherited within our family, it could have consequences for my immediate family and me. But if that was the case, why wouldn't we have already known about it? Surely someone in the family would have recognised this cruel disease if it was inherited by relatives.

Someone suggested that my grandmother's sister, a relative unknown to me, may have had the condition back in the 1970s. So that's where I started looking. The first thing that I did was apply for the death certificates of distant relatives on my grandmother's side. These were not cheap – sixty-five dollars per query. I couldn't afford this on my own, so my mother bankrolled the research. It didn't take long to discover that at least two of my grandmother's siblings had died from MND; however, it was not listed as MND on their death certificates. This revelation was a shock. My heart sank with a great thud. My grandmother's sister Marie Reilly, who lived in Berala, Sydney, died in Lidcombe Hospital on 16 March 1975 at the age of forty, a year after I was born. She had been diagnosed with bulbar palsy two years prior to her death. Bulbar palsy was the same name they used to describe Ashley's MND. For the family-history research, I bought myself a medical dictionary to help me understand the clinical terms. I found out that bulbar palsy means paralysis through the brainstem or bulbar region that controls the muscles for speech, swallowing and chewing. Given the particular set of muscles affected in bulbar palsy, it is no surprise that this form of MND has the worst prognosis of any subtype of MND.

My grandmother's brother James, or Jimmy as everyone called him, also seemed to have died of MND. He was reported to have died from auto muscular dystrophy, which he had suffered from for two years. The term 'auto muscular dystrophy' was likely just a description of what the doctor saw. It would roughly translate to muscle wasting due to an intrinsic dysfunction, as in not caused by external forces. Jimmy died in Brisbane in 1971 at the age of fifty-two.

With Jimmy and Marie dying in 1971 and 1975, respectively, there had not been anyone in the family with MND for two decades. My entire life up until this point, at least. Even then, it would not have been easy to join the dots for the family because twenty years ago they didn't call it MND. It was no wonder that we had no idea that MND was passed on within the family. My next thought was that hopefully we wouldn't see this again for another twenty years. I also thought that I would keep digging back through the family tree to see if there had been similar gaps between cases before that.

When the family found out that I was digging through the family history, an anecdote was passed to me from my grandmother's youngest sister, Barbara, that her mother (my great-grandmother), Daphne, had some weakness in her arms when she died. However, I couldn't find any evidence that she had been diagnosed with any form of MND. Daphne Abrahams died at her home in Merrylands of a heart attack in 1961. She was fifty-three.

My great-aunt Barbara was a tough, warm woman, with a voice that had a roughness that made her sound like a smoker. She was the youngest child and the only one still at home when her mother, Daphne, had died. Although Daphne died of a heart attack, Barbara remembered that her mother's handwriting skills and fine motor skills had declined before her death, and thought that although she did not die of ALS, she may have had it when she died.

As for Barbara, she kept her own condition hidden from her family for three years. It had progressed slowly and she could no longer move her arm above her head. But it was the goitre operation that she underwent that was her downfall. I had not seen Barbara for the time that she had the disease and upon hearing she had it, I was not as surprised as I would have first thought. She died in her sleep in 1998, aged fifty-two, after the operation. Apparently she suffocated. Her son, who was coming from Queensland to see her after he found out about the disease, was too late. She had died while he was travelling down to visit her.

Looking further back, the next definitive evidence of MND in my family was in my grandmother's grandmother and her brother. Mary Ann Barker died in 1930 from progressive muscular atrophy and bulbar palsy at the age of forty-two. Mary's brother Charles Winter died in 1933 from bulbar palsy and asthenia (asthenia is a descriptive term meaning weakness or lack of energy or strength). He was forty-four years old. So, a pattern was emerging through the family where MND clusters of one or two cases were occurring every twenty to thirty years. If the pattern continued, perhaps after Ken and Ashley we wouldn't see another case until after 2015.

The next piece of evidence that I found involved Mary Ann's grandfather George Winter. The trail went cold here but we found out a lot more about George and his last days than we did about successive generations because of the extensive records kept in the era of convict transportation and the fact that the population was so small in the colony of New South Wales that even the most trivial court matters were reported in the newspaper.

George's story ended in January 1882 in Goulburn, the first inland city in Australia. The beginning of the end was when old man George Winter walked towards the brick and sandstone courthouse next to the police station. He gingerly took the few steps into the building. Taking those laboured and tentative steps, he could easily have been mistaken for being drunk, and no one could have been faulted for thinking such a thing, given George's history in this town. George was an average height for the time, five feet five inches, and had a large nose crooked to one side as if it had been broken in a fight. He had a noticeable scar on his throat, a mermaid tattoo on one arm and an anchor on the other that hinted that he worked at sea at some point in his life. His now grey hair looked as though it had once been brown, and his eyes, although tired and weathered, still kept some of their brightness and hazel colouring. On 28 January 1882, Winter felt that he could no longer look after himself, so he gave himself up for the protection of the state at the police court. The court said they would keep him in custody for one week until he could be transferred to a benevolent asylum.

Upon admitting him to prison, it was decided that he was too feeble to stay in gaol, even for the short period it would take to transfer him to the asylum. So much so that he was transferred to the prison hospital the very next day. In the hospital, George was put in the care of the wardsman Edward Rigney, who later recounted their conversation to the coroner. As Rigney was preparing one of the cast-iron beds that were standing at attention in rows like soldiers along the length of the ward, he started a conversation with George. He noticed George's arms were partially paralysed and that he was very weak. Rigney asked George how long he had been like this. George replied that it had been this bad for a few weeks, but he hadn't been right for months if he was honest. George's voice was weak, so he had to repeat himself. Rigney, who noticed an accent, asked George where he came from and how he came to be in Australia. George replied that 'he was born in England, but he had forgotten when he came to Australia'.

This was not really the truth. George had been transported to Australia on the convict ship *Parkfield* when he was twenty-three years old for stealing from someone's house. Although the police never told him what it was that he was supposed to have stolen. He was sentenced to ten years in prison, most of which were served in Australia. He had spent the rest of his life trying to hide these facts, but he could not forget them.

Rigney commented that he seemed well educated. George said that he had been educated in London and could read and write and 'had even given lectures in this colony'.

George got progressively worse until he died a few days later. He was sixty-six. The coroner reported that he died as a result of partial paralysis and prostration or weakness.

Although I cannot say for certain, I have come to believe that George was the first person in our family to have MND. Some modern-day evidence that George may have been the founder event of our family's curse is that the particular genetic mutation in our family is only found in Australia and that the mutation is about two hundred years old. George was born in 1816, placing him at the crime scene both geographically and genetically speaking.

The other area that I thought that I could throw some light on, at the very least for the family, was the question of what causes MND. So, I started reading to find out what was happening in the field of MND research. Whenever I came across a word that I didn't recognise, I would look up the definition and write it in the margins. Pretty quickly, there was no space left in the margins of the papers I read. There are so many field-specific words in scientific papers that it was like reading a foreign language. By learning the language of the neurobiology of MND, I was essentially teaching myself the basics of cell and molecular biology. At some point, I thought it would be helpful for me to do some textbook-style learning, so I had some sense of the entire picture of how a cell works rather than learning what independent components or processes do in relation to MND.

The first test of my newfound knowledge of cell and molecular biology was during a night out for Rachel's friend Christen's birthday. I had a chance to find out what she did working at the Children's Medical Research Institute as a research assistant after finishing her degree in biotechnology. I thought working on childhood cancer was a noble pursuit, and I told her so. She explained that her position was at the bottom of the pile with a lot of repetition and no real autonomy. She was a little disillusioned, but I respected her knowledge and experience as a scientist, and she had always seemed particularly bright. I explained to her my understanding of what I had been reading, and she nodded along in what I took to be solidarity. Still, given that I had not even done high-school biology, it was probably more akin to humouring the guy who had read a few things on the internet. Importantly, my takeaway from the conversation was that I understood what I was reading, which encouraged me to keep reading.

Although I had never heard of MND before Kenny's diagnosis, it started to pop up everywhere now that I heard of it. A friend of

Rachel's mother named Elaine had just lost her husband to MND and, like us, wondered if she should worry about her kids. She invited us around so she could ask me some questions. I explained that most cases were not inherited and that the disease was inherited in a way that it wouldn't skip generations. I also explained what little I knew about the causes of MND. Elaine was very kind and thanked me for answering her questions, and then added that I should go to university to take a few subjects in biology as that would help me with my reading. I had not considered this as an option. It hadn't really occurred to me. But it seemed my basketball career would be coming to a close at the end of 1998 as West Sydney was not taking me on for their national league team, so I decided that perhaps I would give further university studies some thought.

Chapter Six

The Work Begins

Life went on, and in 1998 we had our second daughter, Maddy. Rachel and I originally wanted to call her Fern. But we settled on Maddison. Maddy. She was a baby of the middle of the night. Just as she came into the world in the middle of the night, as a baby she would also keep us awake during the wee witching hours. It was hard work, but both she and Talia were worth it all. Rachel would always say that intelligent babies didn't sleep well, but I would have settled for moderate intelligence and more sleep. Rachel and I took turns getting up with Maddy. From 5am she wouldn't go back to sleep. She didn't really sleep through the night until she was four. By this time, she had worked out that I wouldn't mind if she crawled into bed on my side as long as she didn't wake Rachel. Maddy was a beautiful kid with a cheeky grin and curly white-blonde hair. Her hair was always in tangles and knots, and she didn't like it being brushed. The only person that she would sit with and allow her hair to be untangled by was her gran – my mother.

Maddy had a fantastical imagination, and she was often happiest playing with imaginary people or animals. It was obvious that she was building entire worlds to immerse herself in. Every Tuesday she would spend with her gran, and she would go along with whatever my mother was doing. On one trip to Target, they had finished their shopping and were about to leave when Maddy got upset because she had lost her fairy. My mother didn't remember she had brought a fairy, but it was definitely the kind of thing that Maddy would do, so she started looking for the missing fairy. After a minute or two, staff in the store were offering to help as Maddy was clearly upset. Eventually, there was half a dozen staff helping with the search when Maddy suddenly declared, 'I found it!' She held out her hands to show everyone the toy. In her hands, she held nothing. 'Look, Gran, here is my fairy,' she said. It was then clear everyone was looking for an imaginary fairy. They all had a little chuckle before going back to work.

I loved raising my girls. If I was looking for meaning in life, I know what my mum would have told me: it's about family. Something had to be done.

In 1999, I started looking at the possibility of taking a few biology subjects at the University of Wollongong after Elaine had first suggested it to me. Rachel was very encouraging and has always supported my pursuits regardless of where they might take me. I knew then as I know now that I have always been extremely lucky to have Rachel by my side and I wouldn't have been able to do any of this without her. I have often thought that Rachel deserved better than the life that I could give her.

I made a meeting with the Dean of the Faculty of Science to see if biology studies were possible for me. Rob Norris was a kind man, with greying hair and large spectacles, and was extremely helpful. He walked me through how I could go about enrolling in the subjects. He explained how normally he would expect that someone who hadn't any background in the sciences would complete a bridging course, but in this case he would waive the requirement, and we could see how it went. He signed me up for a Bachelor of Science so that I had the freedom to enrol in subjects that I was interested in.

I initially enrolled in first-year biology and chemistry subjects to see how my studies would go. I would sit up at the back of the lecture hall, quietly listening to lectures while others in the class talked and joked around. I was at a different stage of life to those eighteen-year-old kids. I had to focus on studying in the time I had because when I wasn't in class, I was with my girls or working at the Unanderra post office that my parents had purchased in July 1996. I was well aware that children don't care what assignments you have or what reports you need to write, as long as you give them attention in the moment.

The content was straightforward. Having no formal study of biological sciences prior to these courses, it struck me how much biology was like learning how a machine worked. It was, at least initially, learning about parts of the machine and what they did. For example, the mitochondria are the powerhouse of the cell and they generate the energy currency of the cell, the molecule called ATP. The 'life as a machine' frame of mind suited my brain and the way it works, so from the beginning, I not only understood the science, I excelled at it. I also put this down to the fact that I wasn't studying to pass the class. I was there to understand. I felt that any part of the cell and molecular biology course might come in useful at some stage, so it was important to understand everything.

I did find chemistry a bit more challenging though. I spoke with Rachel's friend Christen who had done the classes five years prior, and her notes really helped me understand the course. The most influential and important part of the first-year subject content was understanding and gaining a proper appreciation of evolution by natural selection. It is such a powerful concept that explains so much about life but with such a simple idea. During those first subjects, the most valuable information that I received came from discussions with the laboratory demonstrators. Their job was to instruct the undergraduate students in the practical component of the course. Typically, this role was filled by PhD students looking for a little extra money and teaching experience, in that order.

Once I had gained confidence in my ability to keep up with the courses, I picked the brains of the PhD students about what research was like at university level and how one would go about such an undertaking. What I took from these conversations was that in order to be able to conduct your own scientific research, first the following list of things would have to be successfully navigated. This list was a road map towards research:

1. Distinction averages across all undergraduate subjects
2. Complete a fourth-year honours project with a first-class grade
3. Apply for and secure a PhD scholarship
4. After four years, complete and graduate with a PhD
5. Secure a post-doctoral training post or fellowship funding
6. Build up some skill and expertise and build a CV that is competitive for funding applications
7. Apply for research funding (application needs to be in the top 15% of all scientific projects).

The whole process would take at least ten years, probably more. It was a valuable and thorough road map for success in academia that would allow someone to do their own research. However, it might as well have been a map of how to climb Mount Everest or instructions on how to get to the moon because I was equally unprepared and ill-equipped to take on such a challenge.

Although I thought there was no chance of doing my own lab research, there was no harm in my using the road map to walk in that general direction. After all, anything that I could learn along the way might be helpful to my family. After the first-year subjects were over, I had scored two distinctions and two high distinctions. This was a very good first step. So, I kept going. I didn't have any high distinctions from my commerce degree, so I was encouraged. Second-year subjects built upon the foundation of the first year, and we delved into particular subjects in more depth. For example, in biochemistry, probably one of the more difficult subjects in the course, we looked at all the biochemical reactions that are used in mitochondria to generate ATP. The fail rate of the subject back then bordered on fifty per cent. I am not sure if this reflected the content of the curriculum or the teaching. One thing I did take away from the subject came from one of my lecturers who said in one particular lecture that although he was using biochemistry in his research and was teaching biochemistry, he was trained in physiology. That stuck with me as a clear indication that regardless of your undergraduate training, you could use that training and still develop and learn skills in another area.

By the time I was studying my third-year subjects in 2002, I surprised everyone, including myself, by getting high enough marks to make the Dean's merit list and achieve second place in biology. While I was taking these subjects, I was still reading papers about the latest MND research. I found a paper that examined how motor neurons were dying in MND. The research was led by Professor Bob Brown at Massachusetts General Hospital. Bob was a neurologist who specialised in ALS, the most common MND, and for many years had flown to Israel to check on particular families with inherited MND that lived in small villages. I respected his dedication to eliminating MND as well as his long-distance house calls. Bob was a kind, softly spoken man with grey hair and a walrus-sized bushy grey moustache, and although he would be a significant player in international MND research for decades to come, this was the first time I had read his work.

When a cell in your body dies, it can do so in an orderly or chaotic fashion. In the same way that the CIA will shred files and destroy computers in advance of leaving an overseas office if time permits rather than evacuating with all the state secrets and other information that could be used against it intact, cells can undergo a programmed cell death that will destroy the DNA and partition off other molecules for safe disposal so that surrounding cells are not damaged. This programmed cell death is called apoptosis, which comes from the Greek word for the falling of autumn leaves. Bob and the team would discover that one can find the molecular signature of apoptosis in the spinal cords of those who have died from MND. This was exciting because perhaps if motor neurons did die from a programmed and orderly process, the program could be stopped. Also, while no one at the University of Wollongong was doing research specifically on MND, I thought perhaps if I was able to do research projects in someone's laboratory on something like apoptosis, I could then potentially relate it back to MND. As it happened, there was someone in the Department of Biology that was conducting research in the area of programmed cell death, and his name was Mark Wilson.

Mark was definitely one of the more interesting and engaging lecturers in the department. What I think made him a better lecturer than most and a great scientist was his ability to cut through the bullshit and get to the point. Although, occasionally, his analogies or hypothetical examples could be a little colourful. He once relayed the following example while talking about physical, biological barriers and how they are the first line of defence against pathogens like bacteria. He said that if he took the entire class and got everyone to strip naked, making sure that you closed your mouth and eyes, and then he stood you in a line while he took a fire hose and sprayed you all with sewage, you would probably be okay. We got the message loud and clear, but at the same time, the imaginary sewage left me feeling soiled.

I wrote to Mark about the possibility of doing an undergraduate research project in his laboratory with the hope that I could start apoptosis research. He agreed to meet me in his office and discuss potential projects. The cell and molecular biology labs were on the top floor of Building 35. It was a brick building with yellow steel window frames and shutters. It must have been built in the 1980s and the university had since moved on with a new coordinated colour scheme, so it stuck out like a sore thumb. To some, it was just known as the yellow building. The design of the building was such that the offices were inside the laboratories. This meant that I had to walk past people doing their lab work to get to Mark's office. The lab benches were full of bottles of clear liquids, tubes in racks, and pipettes hanging on their stands. Notebooks and pieces of paper with calculations and other notes were sprawled over some desks. Little contraptions rotated tubes and rocked containers with rhythmic squeaks like tiny doors were being opened and closed. Something smelled like rotten eggs, only ten times stronger. The shelves that lined every conceivable wall above the benches were filled with canisters of hundreds of different chemicals. Mark's office was in the corner of the lab and contained just his desk, a bookshelf and filing cabinets.

I knocked on the outer door that was propped open with a garbage bin. A student busy at the lab bench pointed to Mark's office. I walked around trying not to touch anything, then knocked on Mark's office door. He gestured for me to come in and sit down.

'Why do you want to do an undergraduate research project?' he asked me.

In retrospect, this is a great question for any potential student and one that I still use today because the motivation behind such a request tells you a lot. While I kept my real motivation to myself at the time, I did convey the desire to work with Mark and his team. Not just for the undergraduate project but for my honours degree as well. Mark was agreeable until I told him that I was interested in working on the apoptosis side of things. He admitted that he was closing down that project and only had one student still actively working on it. He instead offered me the chance to work on another project that he was going to be focusing on. He had been studying a protein called clusterin and had recently discovered that it had similar properties to a group of proteins called molecular chaperones. Chaperones do what the name suggests in that they stop inappropriate interactions between other protein molecules. I was not particularly familiar with chaperone proteins, having not come across them during my undergraduate studies. I said to Mark that I would let him know as soon as possible and thanked him for meeting with me.

I called Mark back the next day and said that I would do the project. I would get to know him well over the next few years. He was a little bit like a cactus, prickly on the outside and soft on the inside once you got past the spikes. A thick skin was a necessary part of being a scientist. While being spiky doesn't make you a good scientist, it helps you to cope with the rejection which is such an ingrained part of research. He was once described by British colleagues as a bull in a china shop because of the contrast of his personality to the diplomatic sensibilities of the Brits. I recall that he had also walked into my office one morning, pointing at me and declaring, 'You're a fucking idiot,' after I had left some piece of equipment on overnight, before turning on his heels and striding away. On the other end of the spectrum, I had heard that he spent hours in the middle of the night chasing away the frogs that were keeping his daughter awake the night before an exam. These qualities made him an excellent scientist, and he was a great mentor to teach me about scientific research through the lens of protein chaperones.

Before we can understand what these protein chaperones are and why they might be needed we must first know what a protein is. To do this it is useful to rewind to the origins of molecular biology. The publication of the paper

'Molecular Structure of Nucleic Acids: a Structure for Deoxyribose Nucleic Acid [DNA]' in 1953 by Watson and Crick, informed by the beautiful X-ray crystallography images produced by Rosalind Franklin, led to a revolution in the way we think about biology. I have imagined their ecstasy and defiant arrogance as they put on their coats and threw a scarf over their shoulders for the short stroll from the Cavendish Laboratory to the Eagle Pub in Cambridge. That chilly February afternoon, they would announce to the patrons of the Eagle that they had won the race to crack the structure of DNA, that they had uncovered the secret of life. I have walked that route along Free School Lane, behind the college grounds of Corpus Christi, dozens, maybe hundreds, of times. As you walk past the sandstone laboratories, click-clacking on the cobblestones, it is hard not to daydream about the early days of biophysics and biochemistry when such famous and infamous personalities were kicking around Cambridge.

One of the fundamental concepts of molecular biology, known as the central dogma, was soon to follow with Francis Crick's publication 'On Protein Synthesis' in 1958. Simply put, the central dogma identifies DNA as the storage of biological information that is communicated in one direction. First, a copy of the segment of DNA, or gene, is made using a molecule called RNA, which acts as a mobile copy of the DNA. From this RNA template, the information is translated into a linear sequence of amino acids, like beads on a string, that makes a protein. Proteins are, in general, the molecules that perform functions in the cell. Humans make around 20,000 different proteins that perform a dizzying array of molecular functions as diverse as providing physical structure, molecular signals, transporting oxygen and catalysing most chemical reactions that occur in the body.

While proteins are initially linear chains, they must take on a particular three-dimensional shape in order to perform their intended function. This fundamental truth of biology – that shape determines function – was gleaned from early experiments such as those from Christian Anfinson at the Harvard Medical School. This concept of protein folding is the same principle that makes a wire coat hanger work. The starting material is a length of straight wire, and although the linear form has no function, once it is folded and twisted into the right shape, it can perform its job of hanging a shirt or coat.

The main job of molecular chaperones is to make sure that a protein makes it to the functional and fully folded form. Without chaperones, proteins would accumulate in misfolded and misshapen forms. We now know that deposits made of accumulated misfolded protein molecules have been found to be a feature of many disease states. The proteins found in such deposits are aggregated together. This is what happens to proteins in egg whites when an egg is cooked. The field of protein aggregation causing disease really began in 1985 when Colin Masters from the University of Melbourne discovered the main component of amyloid plaques from brains affected by Alzheimer's disease. The first time I met Colin was at a conference in 2012. He bounded over to me and, in his bellowing voice, asked gruffly, 'Who are you?' as he reached for my lanyard to take a closer look. 'Ah, Wollongong', he said, as if that was all he needed to know about me. And having found out who I was, he bounded away as fast as he had appeared.

On the other side of the world at the University of Oxford, Professor Christopher Dobson had begun to move his research away from understanding how particular proteins go from being a linear chain or polymer to a folded and functional enzyme and instead towards the growing field that was trying to understand how a functional enzyme could unwind or unfold and form deposits in some diseases. This transition came almost serendipitously when a protein they had been studying, called lysozyme, was found in huge deposits in patients with a particular form of amyloidosis by the esteemed clinician Dr Mark Pepys. For decades to come, students would bet with one another on how long into a lecture Chris would utter the phrase 'literally kilos' of amyloid.

In a theoretical masterstroke and only having worked in the field for two years, Chris would hypothesise that the process of protein aggregation observed in a handful of diseases may not be restricted to the shortlist of proteins associated with disease deposits but that it might be a generic property of all proteins. And that some proteins are more susceptible to this process than others. This insight still informs the work I do today. Chris's genius, I believe, lay in his ability to identify the importance of a particular finding or project with so much clarity. Sometimes this genius could surface during a student's five-minute presentation or, as was the case here when a student came to him with a problem such as 'I accidentally left my protein solution in the instrument over the weekend, and it formed a gel', he wouldn't overlook the mishap but be curious about the result. In this case, the protein was not associated with any disease, yet when they looked at the gel under the microscope, it looked very similar to what was inside the deposits in human pathology.

The presence of molecular chaperones inside cells was first discovered by Ulrich Hartl, a German biochemist. Ulrich is a tall, thin man with grey hair on his head and upper lip, who is softly spoken until after a few wines when he becomes more excitable. He followed us out to a nightclub in Wollongong after a conference dinner one night to the delight of all the students. I first met Ulrich at a conference in Snowmass, in the United States. It was right in the middle of the 2006 FIFA World Cup and as we were both wearing our respective country's jersey, we struck up a conversation.

The molecular chaperones that Ulrich discovered could help a protein go from its unfolded state to its folded and active state. John Carver from the Department of Chemistry at the University of Wollongong was working on a class of molecular chaperones that did not have that folding activity but that could instead prevent the aggregation process. John had suggested that Mark should test the protein clusterin in some of his experiments. The particularly interesting thing about this was that up until then molecular chaperones were known only inside the cell and clusterin was predominantly outside the cell in various fluids.

So a new field of study was born and I fell into it. I knew that there was a growing sense that the deposits of aggregated protein in MND could be responsible for motor neurons dying. It was first proposed by Heather Durham in 1997 and, as is the way with science, the same idea got more traction in the most prestigious journal *Science*, thanks to another researcher, a year later. It hadn't escaped my attention that if these proteins were bad news for the cell, then studying other proteins that could halt the process of aggregation could get me one step closer to doing MND research.

My first-ever project was to determine if there were any other proteins outside of cells that might be chaperones. To do this we went fishing for chaperones using a misfolded protein as bait. While in the project I didn't identify what the putative molecular chaperones were, it was clear that there was a dozen or so proteins in blood that bound to misfolded proteins.

Becoming a scientist changes your view of the world. I think this little project started my brain working differently than it did before. Before, I took everything for granted, and afterwards, I wanted to know how everything worked. I no longer simply took medicines prescribed by my doctor without finding out everything I could about what the drug was and what it actually did in the body. I wanted to know about how humans evolved and how our universe got started. Most of all, I wanted to share that feeling with my daughters so they would grow up in a world that already was filled with that wonder and curiosity. Eventually, my own life would become so entangled with the science I was painstakingly building that it was a part of my identity that couldn't be unpicked.

Chapter Seven

The Promise

It was while I was embarking on my first scientific discovery in 2000 that my mother started having trouble with her left foot. She immediately told us that she thought it was MND. I tried to give her some hope that this could be something else given the back problems that she had experienced in the past. Three vertebrae in her lumbar region had been fused together with four large screws so it wasn't outside the realm of possibilities that her foot issues could have been caused by damage from the degenerating area. However much we hoped that it was nerve damage, it was not to be. It was eventually diagnosed as MND.

The diagnostic process was an agonising and drawn-out affair. The end result was devastating. It wasn't long after Mum's diagnosis that we learned that my mother's sister Kathy had also been diagnosed with MND. Any remaining hope that there might be another twenty-year gap between cases in the family had now been shot down in flames.

Mum kept working at her job at the family post office for some time after the diagnosis. After all, she felt okay and other family members worked there too. That was until the day that she walked to the grocery store to get some lunch and tripped over in the middle of the road. She had to be helped up by passers-by. Having a fall with MND is particularly serious because the limbs are not strong enough to support the head and stop it from hitting the ground. It is for that reason that falls are a major cause of death for people with MND. This fall was scary for all of us and a sign that things were progressing. Mum had some scrapes and bruises and was shaken up but was okay. I had a long conversation with my dad. Things were only going to get worse and he had to consider selling the family post office because someone had to look after Mum. So it was settled and the post office was sold in 2001. My sisters and I had to get new jobs and hunker down for what was in store for Mum.

Out of the blue in mid-2002 we were phoned with the news that my grandmother had gone into hospital. She had pneumonia. Before we even had a chance to think about going to visit, she died. She had kept her MND a secret from everyone and had been having trouble swallowing. She had always blamed herself for passing on the faulty gene to everyone so I think that she thought that somehow she deserved it. She put up no resistance and was gone in the blink of an eye. Her symptoms and rapid decline reminded me of our ancestor George Winter's demise.

Mum wasn't well enough to travel to the funeral so she had dictated a letter for me to read at the service. I packed my suit and Rachel and I drove to Young. When we arrived after the three-and-a-half-hour drive I realised that I had forgotten my shoes. We raced to find a shop that was open and found the Salvation Army had some second-hand shoes for five dollars, but the biggest size was a size ten and I was a twelve. I bought the shoes and somehow squeezed my feet into them but the overwhelming sense of pain clouds my memory of the funeral. All I remember is that I noticed every step as I climbed the stairs to the podium to read my mother's note, and that I tried not to stumble as we carried Nan out of the church and placed her gently in the hearse.

She was much loved and my feet were not the only pain I felt at this moment.

Nan was an amazing woman but you wouldn't have known it by looking at her. She was short – no, tiny. That literally made her the yardstick for all her grandchildren as they grew up. Her hair was grey with white streaks and was always done up in a way that reminded me of Queen Elizabeth II. She had dragged eight kids through some very tough times without much money so she was much respected by the entire family. She was a good sport but was also known for her fair share of shouting at us kids, often as we ran away and into the bush. She would be dearly missed by all of us.

We had barely begun to process Nan's death when another devastating phone call came in August 2002. I was already at work and I was tired even at this early hour of the day. I had woken at 4am after a strange dream where all my teeth had crumbled and fallen out of my mouth.

My mother was in the hospital.

I had received similar calls before, only to receive another call not long after to say that they were out of the hospital and on their way home. So, I didn't panic. My mother had had MND for over two years by this point and needed ventilation. She had felt the need to go into the hospital a couple of times, but we weren't immediately concerned. We had only just seen her a couple of days ago, and she was in good spirits. She loved spending time with the family and was happy just to be alive and with us. She wasn't planning on going anywhere any time soon.

Soon after, I got another phone call to say that this was more urgent than they anticipated. So, we raced as fast as we could to Shellharbour Hospital. I don't remember any of the drive. I couldn't tell you how I got there. I was lost in my thoughts. My mother was a very loving person who always put family first. She was a big part of our lives, and, even in her condition, she could never do enough for us.

What if I am too late? I started to wonder. *I have not had a chance to say goodbye. We haven't even spoken about the possibility. She isn't ready. I'm not ready.*

We rushed into the room where she was being held. The room was small, white and had no windows. It felt claustrophobic. Mum was propped up a little on the hospital bed, her skin a translucent sheen of white. In her nose were oxygen tubes, not the mask that had been attached to her ventilator at home. I rushed to her side. She recognised and acknowledged my presence, but she was too weak to speak.

'I love you. I am here,' I told her as she slipped in and out of consciousness.

'What happened here?' I asked my dad, and he told us how she had had trouble breathing during the night. He had called an ambulance at 4am.

Four am. I reached up and held my jaw, making sure that I had all my teeth in my mouth. This was not a dream.

'Where's the doctor'? I asked, agitated.

A doctor entered. 'Where's her mask?' I then asked.

'It has been taken off because it wasn't providing enough air. She's dying.'

'I know she's dying. She has MND. But not today.' I was getting louder. 'What is wrong with the mask?'

'She is congested, and the nose fitting isn't providing enough air.'

'Let's get a mask that goes over her mouth,' I said. 'That should not be a problem.'

'She's dying,' the doctor repeated.

I was losing my patience with this man.

He didn't have a mask.

'Let me call some other hospitals.' I was pleading now. My heart was racing.

'She is dying,' he said again. 'She is not going home. If you get a mask and she survives past this morning, I will be sending her to palliative care.'

'You don't understand,' I said. 'It is not supposed to be like this.'

The doctor exited, and a wave of fear swamped my body. I felt for my mother's pulse. It was weak, very weak. We didn't have long – maybe minutes.

'Goodbye. I love you, Mum.'

I suddenly felt the chill of the frigid air conditioning in the room.

And then she was gone. Her skin was a yellowy grey, and I could no longer feel her heart.

No. No. No.

The room filled with the wailing of my sisters, and I broke down and sobbed. This was not how it was supposed to be. I was angry. But no amount of anger could bring her back.

I felt lost. I had not ever felt anything like this before. My head was heavy and full of darkness. The kind of darkness that emptied your mind and left a void – a black hole. The kind of darkness that distorted time. Seconds felt like minutes. Minutes felt like hours, stretching the pain out thinly but prolonging it. I felt the weight of responsibility on my shoulders. I should have been able to do something. The doctor hadn't understood our relationship with MND. He was blissfully unaware of the delicate dance that we did with death. It didn't seem right that he got to decide she was going to die that day.

We all went back to 32 Barton Street, all of us exhausted. Weary. I should have been more prepared for this, but I wasn't. At most, she had had a few months left to live. Logically I can see that now, but it still hurts so bad. Sitting in the kitchen in silence with the family, there was a hole in my stomach. A part of me was missing, and it would not be coming back.

Eventually, the familiar warmth of the family kitchen thawed our frozen tongues. Conversations were kindled and we talked about her. She was gone but would never be forgotten. Not by us. We knew we would continue to speak her name and tell one another stories about her. We would pause on her birthday and Mother's Day to think of her. She had had so much love to give, so her death seemed so cruel and senseless.

I found myself wondering what life was all about, what was important. What should we spend our lives doing? Making sure that this didn't keep happening was what I decided. But I didn't say it out loud.

My next thought was about my kids. They loved their gran so much. They would be devastated. Maddy had still been spending one day a week with her. They were particularly close.

Maddy would be four soon. It didn't seem that long ago that we'd walked up to the playground with Talia while Rachel was having contractions. Maddy wasn't born until 2am the next day. Rachel was exhausted. I took Talia to see her new baby sister for the first time the very next day. We stopped in at Woolworths on the way, and Talia picked out a little soft toy duck for the new baby who she wanted to call Molly.

Now, within a six-week period, nearly four years later in 2002, we had lost my grandmother, my mother and my aunt Kathy. It was a shock to all of us. We had never heard of MND before Kenny had it and yet now it was ravaging our family in a way that was beyond anything any of us could have imagined. It was clear that this was not going to stop killing members of the family. It was a wildfire and we currently had no way of fighting it. I knew that the only way to stop this thing was by understanding how MND worked and then using that information to discover therapies that could slow MND progression. This was hard for me to take because I had started down the path to try to understand MND but was so far from being able to help. I had promised my mother that I would do everything that I possibly could to find a cure for this dreadful disease, but I was still so far away from this reality. But instead of succumbing to the growing sense of hopelessness that we all felt, I put all my eggs into the science basket and kept moving forward.

***

After I finished my undergraduate project, I went back to meet with Mark Wilson from the Department of Biology because I knew that there were some funds available. I asked him if he was looking for a research assistant. He was, and I started working part time as a research assistant while I also did my honours project part time. My first job was to purify or isolate certain proteins of interest from human blood serum. I worked up the methods for proteins called haptoglobin and SAP that Mark had identified as possible molecular chaperones, and another protein that I thought had promise called alpha2-macroglobulin. I also optimised a protein isolation protocol for clusterin from the same samples as the other proteins that were being studied in the lab. I worked up a method for using blood serum that everyone could use because up to that point some people in the lab had still been isolating it from semen. No one dared ask where the samples in the freezer came from, but rumours swirled that Mark was supplying them. This speculation led to some of the female students in the lab procuring samples from their boyfriends. My new protocol avoided the whole sticky mess.

For my honours project, I was to test one of these proteins, haptoglobin, to see if it could suppress other proteins from aggregating when under stressful conditions. So the first thing I had to do was to find a few other proteins that would unravel, misfold and aggregate under mild conditions, like 42 degrees Celsius. This project really set me on the path to studying protein aggregation. I had to get moving because I didn't want to sit by again while MND took the lives of my family members and not be able to do something. I was unusual among my peers in that I was partially supervising the other honours students as I was undertaking the same degree. In the end, I achieved first-class honours in 2004, which allowed me to apply for a PhD scholarship.

I was another step closer. I had taken my first step along the road using the map that I had drawn to take me towards doing my own research.

Chapter Eight

The Unwelcome Member of the Family

My cousin Stacey was twenty-six, she had two small children to the man she loved, Dave, and she was getting married. It was November 2004. We had driven outside of the Young township to the grounds of an elegant estate and garden to watch them tie the knot. The homestead was a double-storey mansion surrounded by large arches and balconies that would not have been out of place in the English countryside. The house was surrounded by gardens with large established trees. If the house was the same age as the trees, it must have been well over one hundred years old.

Although we had driven out of town, we did not escape the heat. It was the type of day where the air had the same overwhelming heaviness under the shade of a tree as it did out under the blazing sun. Stacey looked beautiful. She was tall and slender with long blonde hair and a square face that could be fierce, but today was soft and welcoming. The elegant white dress somehow made her look taller. There was not a dry eye among the guests as she gracefully walked down the aisle with her father, Allen.

Stacey had been diagnosed with MND only a few months ago, so today was bittersweet.

Stacey had lost her mother, Kathy, her grandmother and her brother Ashley to MND in the last seven years. She knew all too well how this would play out. She wasn't alone. We all had a sense that MND had rounded us up and was picking us off one by one. It truly was a beast. But there was a little hope for the family. There were scientists in the USA, such as Bob Brown and Don Cleveland, who had been working on a gene-silencing therapeutic explicitly made for families like ours with mutations in the SOD1 gene. Despite our genetic misfortune, it seemed as though there was a little light at the end of the tunnel. Although, in all honesty, the tunnel was extremely long and the light very dim. The genetic cause of our family's curse was a mutation in the SOD1 gene. Because it was the first genetic mutation found to cause MND, it was also the most studied gene. I hoped that this head start would translate to faster development of therapies for our family.

At the turn of the new millennium, the rumblings of a scientific revolution were on the horizon, and MND researchers were right there hoping to ride the wave. If the revolution, which would come to be known as gene silencing, was a tsunami, then the first ripples of evidence came in the mid-eighties with a swathe of mysterious and sometimes apparently contradictory findings, but none more striking than the mystery of the purple petunia. While working for a small biotech company called Advanced Genetic Sciences, geneticist Richard Jorgensen attempted to genetically manipulate a purple petunia to make it extra dark purple to attract the attention and perhaps financial investment of venture capitalist groups.

Jorgenson and his colleagues knew which gene produced purple pigment in petunias and thought it reasonable to conclude that additional copies of the gene should make the flowers darker. However, when they added extra copies of the purple pigment gene, the modified plant had white flowers instead of making darker flowers. It seemed like the plant was totally devoid of purple pigment. The pure white flowers seemingly defied all logic because even if the added copies of the gene were somehow incorrect, the plant should still have its initial level of purple. It was as if the modification had deleted all the purple genes, including the original naturally occurring genes.

A decade later, researchers Andrew Fire and Craig Mello had discovered that cells had evolved a cellular defence mechanism against viral invaders to stop them reproducing or incorporating their genes into the genome. This process can identify specific forms of RNA that it considers foreign and destroy them. Not only will it destroy the initial RNA molecule, but it keeps a little piece of the RNA to use as a comparison so that it can rapidly identify that particular RNA sequence and destroy it. So the petunia plant must have recognised the additional gene as foreign and silenced all copies of the gene. Very quickly, it was apparent that this mechanism could be tricked or hijacked into destroying any gene, even one of the cell's own genes, if fed a well-designed small RNA molecule. This has been extremely useful as a tool in biological research since it allows researchers to see what happens when you turn a gene off. Even more importantly, it can be used as a therapeutic strategy in the case of diseases where it would be advantageous to switch off a faulty gene. In general, we call this process RNA interference or RNAi. Essentially it is gene silencing, and Fire and Mello would win the Nobel Prize in Physiology or Medicine for its discovery in 2006.

It was easy to see why there was so much excitement about gene silencing in MND circles. The SOD1 gene that causes MND is a perfect candidate for this type of silencing because it damages motor neurons by a toxic gain of function. That is, the mutant SOD1 gene causes MND by accumulating too much of the misfolded SOD1 protein, not by a lack of the protein or the enzyme activity it would typically perform.

Very soon after the discovery of RNAi, two distinct camps appeared that were designing RNA molecules to silence the mutant SOD1. This was an extremely attractive therapeutic strategy because it doesn't rely on an understanding of how the mutated gene causes damage to motor neurons resulting in MND, just that too much of it is bad news. The first experiments to test that RNAi could reduce the amount of SOD1 inside living cells were conducted by a team led by Bob Brown. Another study, led by Don Cleveland and Tim Miller, followed shortly after and showed that these small interfering RNA molecules could be delivered using a virus that had been engineered to deliver the RNA but could not reproduce itself. His results showed that the RNAi resulted in some modest improvement in muscle strength in the mice it was tested in. While these pioneering studies showed that SOD1 protein level could indeed be reduced, the RNAi used, in this instance called small interfering RNA, has since been superseded by molecules that have proven more effective. Indeed, within twelve months, Don Cleveland and co would switch to a molecule called antisense oligonucleotide or ASO.

Stacey and Dave were able to get in touch with Bob Brown through the producers of the TV show *60 Minutes*, who were doing a story on Stacey. We watched along with the rest of Australia.

In nervous anticipation, Stacey and Dave sat together on their blue sofa waiting for Bob to call. The phone rang, and they glanced at each other briefly before picking up the handset. During the phone call, Bob did most of the talking, telling them that so far his results looked promising. 'But can we move from a mouse to humans in twelve or eighteen months? That is the big question,' he said.

In her heart, Stacey knew the answer was no but clung on to the possibility that there was still a chance. Her husband, Dave, understood with a certain amount of clarity, that this was now a race between Stacey's disease progression and the development of Bob's therapy. He worried that if they lost the race, it might be by just months. Stacey articulated the situation with precision when she said, 'There is still a chance. Not a great chance, but still a chance.'

Stacey continued to get worse, and the drug trial never came. She died in July 2006 hoping that the cure would come one day, hopefully in time for her two daughters.

For me, this was another gut punch, but sadly I had started to become numb to all the death. We had somehow come to accept MND within our family. It was unwelcome and feared but a part of the family nonetheless. I was still not working on motor neurone disease, and, in general, I was finding research a slow grind. I had to pick myself up again. I had to keep my eyes steady on the long game and hope that MND didn't do too much more damage in the meantime.

I also had to think strategically. It was becoming clear that to get where I wanted to be, I could not just complete a PhD, but I would need to position myself as one of the country's most promising emerging scientists. Funding for research was becoming increasingly scarce, and only the top fifteen per cent of applicants were being funded. Not the top fifteen per cent in the field of MND but the top fifteen per cent in all fields of research combined. I would need to work hard, very hard, if I was even to have a chance. Even then, I knew that my chances were slim. I would also need to be smart in the way I worked and only place my efforts where they would advance my career. On top of all that I would need a large dollop of luck. As far as I could tell, success would mean publishing papers and also having some scientific reputation and impact. So I set about working hard and becoming known. A face that people could put to a name when they read my funding application.

It was logical for me to keep working with Mark Wilson for my PhD. The projects were related, and I thought he was an excellent scientist. His science was rigorous, and he was blunt when he needed to be. He would not mince words. He would tell you straight up if something was poorly designed or was missing something important. That is what I needed. I didn't have time to dwell on anything. I just needed to keep moving forward. However, although Mark had great ideas for projects and was a good scientist, he was not particularly successful with grant applications. I think the one thing that hurt Mark with his funding applications was his lack of extensive networks in the field, which is crucial for success. Not that I was a master communicator by any stretch of the imagination, but I knew I would have to learn this skill – and fast.

When I got working, I could be very single-minded. Like the day I was supposed to pick Talia up from school and was lost in some experimental work away from my office. The school called me, but I didn't receive the messages. By the time I got to school, Talia was in tears, and all of the other students had gone, and so too had most of the teachers. I never was that late again, partly because I felt so bad but also because Rachel made me get a mobile phone to make sure that I was contactable at all times.

Even with everything going on, Rachel remained the most significant influence in my life. I had become more comfortable in my skin, and it was all due to Rachel holding my hand and helping me be a more confident and outgoing individual. I still had times when crowds of people overwhelmed me, but I no longer felt that I had to sit quietly in a corner somewhere to avoid conversation. This was a handy everyday skill for social settings but would prove vital for increasing my presence at work.

I had always kept my fears of developing MND to myself. It was a painful thing to talk about, especially with Rachel. She had started having nightmares that everyone around her would die and that she would be alone. She wouldn't let me say to her that it wouldn't be like that. She knew that I couldn't promise that, no matter how hard I worked. It was my worst fear as well, and talking about it wouldn't make it go away. It just brought all the possibilities to the front of our minds and made it difficult to live a normal life. I had also started having nightmares. Always being chased by something or someone that I couldn't see. It didn't need much dream weaving to see that MND was hunting me down.

Mark had received some funding to strengthen ties with the lab of Christopher Dobson at the University of Cambridge. He used part of the funding to send me to Cambridge for six weeks. It was a life-changing trip for me. Not because of the science but because of the friends I would make and because I fell in love with the city. When I wasn't in the laboratory working with Janet, one of Chris's postdoctoral researchers, I was wandering the streets taking in the centuries-old architecture of the colleges, the bookshops and the green spaces. When I first started to explore, the whole city felt like a museum curated by the likes of Isaac Newton, Watson and Crick, Stephen Hawking, Jane Goodall, Dian Fossey and Dorothy Hodgkin. I was used to a campus with a border delineating university and town, but Cambridge University departments and colleges were scattered throughout the city and could be surrounded by houses, schools or even pubs. Walking around Cambridge with the cobblestones underfoot, discussions of discovery on the lips of people walking by, the scent of college gardens in the air and the sense of the intellectual giants propping up the foundations of the city were alluring and hypnotic. I was in my element.

Nearing the end of my stay, one of the team members threw a party, in a tiny pink cottage with a thatched roof. The doorways were made for people of a different era when diet and health care affected stature such that I had to remember to duck under the doorway every time. I soaked up the atmosphere. I met an interesting character whose name was Giorgio. He was Italian but had done his PhD in Sweden. He was very interested in what we could potentially test in cells. He had this idea about how the proteins formed aggregates and how this might make them toxic to cells. We chatted for hours, and I didn't even make it into the main room of the house.

Before leaving Cambridge, I went to the bookstore Heffers and scanned the popular science shelves for a book to read on the way home. I thought that the book *Darwin and the Barnacle* looked interesting and it was written by a Cambridge local, Rebecca Stott. I had finished it before we landed in Sydney. My main takeaway from the book was that Darwin had formulated his theory of natural selection very early on but had seen how the scientific community reacted to novices proposing theories of evolution. He wanted to be taken seriously. He decided to do two things. The first was to work extremely hard and put together so much evidence that it was hard to argue against, and the second was to build up a reputation as a scientist of repute. He did this in a field that was not directly related to evolution. He decided to put together a family tree and naming system of barnacles. I immediately understood what he had set out to do, and I appreciated the beauty of the strategy. I knew then that I would have to continue working in this other field of molecular chaperones to learn how to be a scientist and build a real reputation before coming clean to everyone that I really just wanted to get on with my own MND research.

I applied for an international fellowship from the Australian Research Council (ARC) when I was finishing my PhD. The project was to continue working on a protein that I had discovered could act as a molecular chaperone called alpha-2-macroglobulin. I thought that a year in Cambridge would be invaluable training and would be an amazing experience. I had submitted another three applications for various schemes because I didn't know how competitive I would be. The future of my ability to keep doing research was now out of my hands and in the hands of a panel of experts.

DREAM JOURNAL: 19 JULY 2006

I am swimming on a beach with Rachel and the kids when, all of a sudden, missiles start crashing into the water. I struggle to find the kids and yell for Rach to take shelter behind the large rock shelf. We shelter there for quite a while, all the time wondering if we will live through this ordeal. Large banging waves, explosions splash as the large missiles crash into the water.

Chapter Nine

Our World Crumbling Once More

Around the time Stacey was ill, my sister Sarah and her husband, Jayson, along with their baby son, Logan, had moved back to the Wollongong area after a few years in the far north of Queensland. Jay was in the navy and had completed his post, and had come back to work in the hydrographic office. After their second child, Hannah, was born, Sarah had applied for a job with the Australian intelligence agency ASIO and had made it to the interview stage. She was explaining to me that she wasn't supposed to say anything about the interview but I kept asking questions. As we were talking the phone rang and so I said jokingly, 'That's probably ASIO because we are talking about them.' It was. We had a good laugh.

In 2007, Sarah was accepted into the air force and had to spend three months training in Melbourne before receiving her posting. She would leave Jay with their two beautiful kids, Hannah and Logan, while she trained. She started running to increase her fitness so that she would be ready for the training.

It was while she was running that she noticed something wrong with her foot. She went to the physiotherapist to get it checked out because it was affecting her times. She was told by the physio that he thought it was probably nerve damage and that she should see a neurologist. This news set alarm bells ringing and we all feared the worst.

We all piled into the neurologist's office that was inside a new building attached to the hospital on the campus of Macquarie University. The corridors and doorways in the neurologists' rooms were wide to accommodate assistance and wheelchairs but I was not sure a group as big as ours had come along as support before. The neurologist, Professor Dominic Rowe, called us a scrum to cut the tension that hung so heavy in the air.

Dom had been Mum's neurologist after we'd 'shopped around' after finding previous neurologists rude and arrogant. A short man with a head of thinning, grey hair, he has a sharp intellect and an equally sharp tongue that makes you glad that he's on your side. His trademark is a bow tie. So much so that he is occasionally not recognised immediately without it. Dom is down to earth though, and makes you feel that he is in your corner, not in a different corner watching from arm's length. He has a spacious corner office overlooking the hospital with a desk close to the door, a hospital bed to the left and a few chairs opposite both. A large sculpture made from rusted iron sits on his desk; presumably, it represents something related to the brain.

That day, he brought in some additional chairs to seat our scrum. Along with Jayson and me, Sarah had also brought our sister Naomi and Dad. We all knew the gravity of the situation.

After some attempts at light-hearted conversation, we settled into the business of what we came for. Dom proceeded to ask Sarah some questions and examined her legs. Push down, pull up, move this, push against that. He also tested her reflexes. To my surprise, after a short examination, Dom returned to his desk.

'We have to assume it's the beastie...'

We were all taken aback. So quickly, our world was crumbling once more, and we would never stand on solid ground again. Jay and Sarah sat quietly holding hands. The news was soul-crushing and I couldn't help but think about their beautiful kids, who were only four and two years old at the time.

I immediately brought up the possibility of a drug that might be helpful. A medication that was once used for malaria had been shown to reduce the level of the SOD1 protein, achieving similar results to that of RNAi gene silencing. The drug had been patented in 2006 by Sean Scott, who had started the ALS Therapy Development Institute in the United States. He also had the same mutation to SOD1 in his family so was equally motivated to find a treatment for SOD1-associated MND. I had pre-empted the diagnosis and had scoured the literature for something that might be effective and available right away. The RNAi and antisense therapies looked promising but sadly they were still no closer to human trials; nothing much had progressed since Stacey's diagnosis and subsequent death. I was desperate to help. I didn't want Sarah to slip through my fingers as well.

Dom agreed to try the malaria medication on compassionate grounds and to monitor Sarah's progress closely. My plan was to bring Sarah into the lab in Wollongong every month and take some blood to see if the dose of pyrimethamine was at least reducing the level of SOD1 in her blood cells. We took a sample before she started so that we could tell if it was decreasing. I didn't know how I would cope if it didn't work.

Sarah was my baby sister. She had a cute round face with red hair, freckles and a smile that could light up a room. To use a well-worn cliché, she was the life of the party. She always made any boring event a lot of fun. I loved her a lot. She was also the stereotypical last child. She was spoiled by everyone, given everything on a platter and was allowed to do things that I would never have been permitted to do. Not that I am complaining. I also had a soft spot for her, and she was too cute to ever be angry at. The only time that my patience wore thin was when she had an injury or a cold. She was not very good at being sick, and I don't know if it was because she just wasn't very resilient or that she knew that Mum would baby her. Probably the latter.

My first memory of Sarah is from when she was still growing in our mother's womb. I remember being called into the kitchen and told to sit down: 'There's something we need to tell you.' As a kid who was in Year 2, there were only a limited number of things rattling around in my head, so I had no idea what this talk could possibly be about. I knew from the tone of Mum's voice it was serious, so I was thinking about things that were my worst nightmare, things like that we had to move house away from all of my friends. I didn't even consider that Mum or Dad or any relatives could be sick or dying. I hadn't experienced anything like that in my whole lifetime. I wish now that our kids could be in that same space, a place built with high, safe walls to hide them from the realities of our family's world. A place where they didn't have to worry about who was going to be sick next. But the news my mum and dad were telling me wasn't sad. We were going to get a new brother or sister. I'm not sure how I felt exactly. I wasn't sad but I wasn't over the moon either. I really was hoping for a little brother, though.

I took Sarah to school for 'show and tell' as soon as she was home from the hospital. I remember the classroom. It was a demountable, green with large windows. I was very familiar with one of the corners of the room since I had been sent there more than once. The teacher finally said I could bring her in, so I was able to go out into the playground and get Mum to bring her inside. I was so proud, as if I had just whipped her up from scratch at home. I am still proud of her. She reminded me so much of Mum, and it brings a smile to my face when I think of her. I remember being allowed to hold her. She was so small. Just a bundle of pink skin, with little arms and legs, and a big head, although her head was mostly cheeks. It was the first thing everybody said: chubby cheeks. They stayed with Sarah for years. It didn't seem that long ago that she was that small and helpless, and I had to be reminded to keep a hand under her neck so her head didn't fall back. I find myself now thinking that I was doing the same thing when she was sick – trying to hold her without hurting her and remembering to be careful not to let her head fall. The difference was that back when she was a baby, although she was helpless, she didn't know any different. When she had MND, her helplessness was fully understood, and it added to her pain.

Every time I think of Sarah, there is one moment in time that I recall from the deepest, darkest parts of my brain. This moment is linked with her name, and I think that it is what my brain has frozen in time. It was a happier time. She was about two or three. Her hair was not long enough to put into a ponytail and had a kind of wave in it. Of course, her hair was strawberry (I think that is the polite way to put it) in this image. She was moving away from me along the concrete path, which was bordered by freshly mown green grass. The smell of freshly cut grass mingled with the pungent spent mower fuel. Although she was moving away from me, she turned slowly and gave me a cheeky grin. It was like she was saying that 'I'm going over here now, but I want to know you are watching'. At that moment, in early 2008 when she was getting ever sicker, I felt like that she was moving away from us, although this time it was not through her own devices. Although it was hard for her and for us all, she still had that cheeky grin. I wanted her to know we were still watching her, and we loved her, and that we wouldn't ever let her out of our hearts.

To my despair, Sarah stopped taking the pyrimethamine. She didn't feel that it was working, and it made her feel sick. I was devastated. I had failed again, and every time I opened the freezer door in the laboratory, there were her samples that we had originally taken staring out at me, stabbing me in the heart. I didn't know if I had the energy to keep going. But I had to. I still hadn't even finished my PhD. It felt like the road ahead was too damn long and that I would never make it. With a heavy heart laden with the loss of so many and the expectation of so many more, I trudged forward.

One foot in front of the other. One step at a time.

Of all the fellowship applications I submitted, it was the twelvemonth international fellowship that was successful. I was awarded the fellowship to train as a postdoctoral fellow at Cambridge University under the tutelage of Professor Chris Dobson in 2008. It provided the only funds that I had to keep researching after my PhD. Although I had tried to publish as many papers as possible to make myself competitive, in the end I think it was a combination of good luck and the reputation of Chris that got me over the line. When Sarah found out, though, she vetoed the plan. She thought that she might only have a couple of years to live and didn't want us to spend a large chunk of it overseas away from her. She was right, of course. So I asked the ARC if I could push back the start date on compassionate grounds. They agreed to a twelvemonth delay, something that we could then re-evaluate at the end of that period. Fortunately for me, Mark Wilson had accepted a position as Associate Dean, leaving a twelve-month teaching position available in my department at the University of Wollongong. In contrast to the way this type of role would be filled nowadays, with casual or part-time teaching filling the void, Mark was able to recommend me for the role and secure me a full-time teaching and research position for twelve months. It was a huge relief.

We made sure we visited Sarah every week and other times when needed. She was very well loved by her friends, so every day there was someone around to spend time with her or to help Jay or the kids. Even early in Sarah's disease, she had remarked that she could feel a new loss of muscle every day. It was moving particularly fast, which was not a good sign.

In a very generous act, there was a donation of a trip to Disneyland for Sarah, Jay and the kids. After hearing of this, my dad decided to pay for everyone else in our family to go with them on a road trip on the West Coast of the United States. Sarah really wanted to go to Las Vegas so we booked a trip from Los Angeles to Vegas to San Diego. It was a great trip. Sarah's legs were too weak to walk any further than a few steps so we pushed her around everywhere in the wheelchair. She did manage to get on a few rides at Disneyland. I took Sarah and Logan on the whitewater rapids ride. Although it was a kids ride, it was definitely the scariest ride that I experienced over the three days. There were no seatbelts in the log boats and I had Sarah in my lap. She focused on holding on to Logan, which meant I had to hold on to her. She was sliding around everywhere and I tried my best to hold on tight. I shed a few tears on that ride as I realised that I would not be able to hold on to her forever.

I didn't really have any alternatives for a drug that might slow Sarah's disease progression. She had come to terms with it and let go. The free fall was dizzyingly fast. We were in the United States in October and November 2007, only three months after the scrum had walked into the neurologist's office, and by February 2008 things were bleak. Sarah's voice was a combination of raspy and breathless, which is a signpost that points to the beginning of the end in MND. It was happening so fast that there was no time to organise equipment to lift her out of bed or to provide any support apart from the BiPAP ventilator to help her breathe. On our visits I would give Jay a break and get anything and everything she needed. I would have to carry her to the toilet when she needed to go. It was heartbreaking.

Hannah and Logan were too little to understand what was happening but Sarah loved them a lot. More than a lot — she loved them as much as anyone has ever loved another person. In her last weeks, she recorded video messages for them. I wish that her kids had had more time with Sarah. To understand how much she loved them and to make some memories that they could cherish.

Sarah told us that there would come a time that she could go no further and that she would go out on her terms. And that she would give us some warning. Of course, this put us on tenterhooks and every phone call from Jay would set my heart racing and my head spinning.

It was 4am when Jay rang. All I remember was he said, 'It's time.'

We jumped into action. We called our friend to come and look after the kids and then we rushed to 32 Barton Street. Sarah was with Jay, in Mum and Dad's old room at the front of the house. It was a direct right turn as soon as you walked in. I looked up at the portraits of us as babies, wishing that we could rewind to happier times. The sadness was palpable and hung heavy in the air. We took turns with Jay, my dad and Naomi to say our goodbyes. Rachel and I entered the room. Sarah was propped up with pillows in the double bed opposite the bedroom door. The large aluminium-framed window had the blinds drawn. Sarah had the mask of the BiPAP ventilator over her nose, which was red raw from so much use. She was thin, too thin. She was exhausted, weary. Clearly, she had had enough.

We told her how much we loved her and how much she meant to us. We held her hand tight.

'Promise me.' Her voice was so soft I could barely hear it over the ventilator. 'Promise me you will watch over the kids.'

We were all in tears. It was time to let her go.

After we said our goodbyes, Jay went back in. He held her until the end. We all sat in the kitchen and waited. Jay emerged and we gave him a hug. Our baby sister was gone.

***

Although we felt the loss of Sarah keenly and in some ways it was more tragic than losing Mum, the process of my sister's death was less traumatic. Sarah had taken the unknown element out of the equation. She was prepared. Even to the extent that she had made slide shows for the funeral. It also gave us the opportunity to get ready for her death. Sarah took control back from MND, which had been ravaging her body – one last defiant moment to go out on her own terms. I respected her for that, and I was immensely proud of how she approached her life as well as her death. I will not let MND define her.

We all rallied around Jay. His world had just been shattered into pieces and he had two little kids to look after, so there was no time to grieve. Jay is a good man and he has done a great job raising Hannah and Logan. Sarah would be proud.

Sarah's death was particularly hard to take. I think mostly because I had always felt protective of her. That came from all those years of taking Sarah's side in sister–sister arguments with Naomi. I always felt that Naomi could look after herself so it was only natural that I'd take Sarah's side. I felt, perhaps wrongly, that she was helpless. Right then, though, as she was dying, I was the helpless one. I had been a student for eight years and I hadn't been able to do any of my own laboratory research yet. It was too slow. I had to live with the fact that I was not able to do anything for Sarah. But I told myself that I would keep my promise to Sarah and I would make sure that I could do something that would protect those beautiful kids of hers, Hannah and Logan. I needed to work even harder.

DREAM JOURNAL: 16 APRIL 2007

I am being chased by unknown people in dark clothes. I am protecting a child (8–10 years old). The child has no particular identity – only I fear for their safety.

We are chased through a series of buildings, hallways, windows onto corrugated iron rooftops, where we scamper away from the chasers. Many times over we are almost caught and each time I am able to fend them off, from a distance since they carried guns. I am using some sort of magical power, maybe a push through the air, like on the kids show 'The Avatar' or like Jedi mind powers.

As usual we are chased for what seems like hours and, as always, I wake up tired from the experience.

Chapter Ten

The Clock Starts Ticking

When asked, I always recommend anyone to hold off from being genetically tested for inherited MND. Unless there is good reason of course, such as potential treatment availability or for family-planning purposes. There is something to be said for having a sliver of hope that you don't carry the MND-causing mutation compared to the overwhelming sense of dread and futility that comes with knowing that you have a genetic lesion that will cut your life short in such a torturous manner. But I did not heed my own advice. I thought that if I had the test and it was all clear then I could give my girls an opportunity to grow up outside the repressive shadow of MND. However, this plan did not come to fruition.

I do not have very clear memories of the genetic test I took in 2007. I presume my consistent lying over many years about taking the test somehow buried the memories so deep that they are no longer retrievable. I am not a very good liar so it worked in my favour to bury those memories deep in the furthermost recesses of my mind. I cannot count the number of times that I was asked about my genetic status in media interviews. It was easiest to say that I had not had the test. I felt the most uneasiness lying to our kids about it, but I understand that the knowledge of my status would have brought MND into our home and we had enough problems with it already knocking on the front door. To be honest, I had trouble telling untruths to the kids even about some apparently innocuous things like Santa Claus and the Easter bunny. I always felt that they trusted me to tell the truth and one day they would find out I hadn't always been completely honest and they would no longer trust me.

I remember that I took a blood test locally and had it sent off to the lab. I thought that my GP would get the results but it wasn't that simple. They made me go to Concord Hospital to meet with a neurologist, a geneticist and a genetic counsellor. Rachel and I sat there in silence as they gave us the news. I did carry the genetic mutation that resulted in one amino acid change at position 148. V148G. I felt numb. Like I was outside looking in, watching this unfold on someone else. How could this be? It wasn't supposed to be like this — I was supposed to be able to tell my girls that they didn't have to worry anymore. I started to wonder how accurate the test was and what the probability was that I actually had the mutation. But the reality was that the chances were so very high that it might as well be a certainty.

We found ourselves walking to another building along timber boardwalks. Concord

Hospital was built as a repatriation hospital for returning soldiers and is a campus of smaller buildings joined by covered walkways. We arrived at the office of the genetic counsellor and I was already resenting this appointment that we had agreed to. The counsellor tried to explain what the test results meant. I already knew. Probably with more clarity than he could provide. He told us that it didn't mean that I had motor neurone disease. I told him I knew that. He tried to tell me the average age of onset. I didn't bother to tell him that his statistics meant nothing. Ashley was twenty-one and my grandmother was seventy-two. I just wanted him to stop talking so I could go home with Rachel and she could hold me.

We agreed not to tell anyone. Especially not the kids.

Rachel was still having nightmares about losing everyone she loved to MND. It was her worst fear. This too could have been removed from her dreams and replaced with a lightness that we had not known for years if the results had been different. I wanted nothing more than to be able to tell Rachel that we were free from this wretched curse. Instead I told her that the science was progressing and that one day there would be a cure. I would make sure of it. She looked up at me with a sadness in her eyes so deep that I didn't know if it had an end. 'You can't promise me that,' she said.

And she was right.

DREAM JOURNAL:
6 AUGUST 2008

We are having a picnic lunch on a grassy area. The area is rectangular in shape and is bordered by trees and some buildings, made by bricks. There are many people. Although I notice no one in particular I know it is my family – although I feel Rachel is there, somehow I do not feel that Talia and Maddy are there.

During the lunch the clouds come over very quickly – dark clouds like a titanic-sized storm is on its way. It starts to rain but soon after it starts to hail; not just normal hail stones but ones as big as a soccer balls hurtling through the sky. People scatter everywhere. I notice that the hail stones are coming from a particular direction and so I run in that direction, noticing that they are flying in at about forty-five degrees. I remember distinctly watching these huge hail stones coming crashing towards me as I run. I make it to a brick wall structure and watch the stones crash on the ground (they could not get me because of the angle); however, some of the family don't go in this direction. In particular, two people are caught in the storm. I race out to them. One has been hit by a stone on the head and is bleeding profusely. I don't think he is going to make it but I carry him to the wall where I lay him down. He isn't in good shape but still alive.

Chapter Eleven

Cambridge

As we approached the Free Press Pub, the sounds of scores of voices filled the cool, crisp air. The noise, seemingly amplified by the walls of the pub, sounded like the bubbling of water over rapids. Laughter mingled with happy conversations. The occasional raucous voice broke through the chatter so it could be understood. We were rugged up in layers of jackets, woollen scarves and beanies over the top like fabric wedding cakes. It was, after all, January in England. I reminded the girls that these people we were meeting were my new colleagues so they needed to be on their best behaviour. The Free Press was one of the many pubs in Cambridge that were only a short stroll along the narrow streets lined with terraced houses from the place we were renting. Our temporary home was in the quiet Covent Garden, off Mill Road, backing on to Fenner's Cricket Ground. The pub was a free-standing building made from a light yellowy coloured brick, with white cottagestyle framed windows and a small, black lean-to entrance to allow punters to enter without letting the frigid winter air inside.

As we entered, the volume of the voices jumped as they tried to push past us and escape out the door and into the starry night. Inside, the din of voices bouncing off the walls and the ceiling confused the senses so that it was impossible to say for certain which voice came from which direction. The scene before us was one of a Dickensian portrait of an alehouse with the room filled with animated faces crowded around tables all warmed by the flames in the open fireplace. What brought this scene out of the Victorian era and into the present was the existence of North Face snow jackets hanging on the backs of chairs and the ever-present glow of mobile phones lighting up the faces of those messaging friends. The room seemed small with the crush of tables and chairs and the low ceiling. Beer swayed and sloshed in pint glasses occasionally raised. The members of the Dobson group that we were there to meet were across the room, and as we made our way across they set to work making space for us, their voices a chatter of accents from Italy, France, Spain, America and, of course, Britain.

I had only met some of the group in passing so I was a little nervous. In truth, I was looking forward to our stay in Cambridge. Cambridge! I had to pinch myself. I was going to be researching in the Chemistry Department at the University of Cambridge. Many of the buildings in the colleges and around town had not changed since the days of Isaac Newton and the modern university had a higher density of Nobel Prize winners than anywhere in the world. The journey from Oak Flats to Cambridge is about as far as one could travel, both figuratively and literally. And although this stay in Cambridge was not the final destination of my research journey, just a short stop along the way, we would use it as a reset button and an escape from our lives back in Australia. Not one person here knew about my family background and that was refreshing. It was as if the weight that I bore got a little lighter. We could spend this time focusing on our little family and step out of the shadow of MND, albeit temporarily.

We made quite an impression that night, courtesy of Talia and Maddy. The general squirminess of our kids somehow managed to spill a glass of red wine onto someone's white knitted jumper. The wine had been temporarily placed back on the table mid-conversation and after the table was bumped it had ended up all over a woman named Bennedetta. I was extremely embarrassed and apologetic. I wanted to buy a new glass of wine and give some money to Benne to have her jumper cleaned but she would not have it. She said not to worry as she had many little cousins and knew what kids were like. Although I was worried about this introduction, in the end, I would have no reason to be anxious and Benne would end up playing an important role in my Cambridge story.

Throughout the remainder of 2008, after Sarah's death, I had floated like a ghost. I tried hard to hold onto all of my memories of Sarah, but they wouldn't stay.

The mind is cruel like that. It's like trying to hold the beach in your hands: eventually, the sand and water will slip through your fingers no matter what you do. So I have tried with all my might recently to reach back into the corners of my mind to remember everything about Sarah. I was surprised to find that I didn't have as much stored in my mind as I had hoped. My head is hurting from its struggle to remember everything she had been, everything she had done and said. It's like my brain is squeezing tight to hold onto every little thing. So I thought that if I wrote these things down, my head would stop hurting for a little while. This, of course, will not stop my heart from hurting. I'm not sure that it ever will.

A lot of my time for the remainder of 2008 was taken up by teaching at the University of Wollongong. It's not that I didn't like teaching. In fact, I particularly enjoyed the face-to-face aspects of teaching and found the students to be engaged and keen to learn. Although, I did discover that some students were perhaps a little too keen to do well in my classes. One night I was out at a bar with some friends and a young woman approached me and said, 'My friend over there takes your class.' She pointed to a group of young people.

'Okay?' I replied.

'She really, really wants good marks in the final exam. And I will do anything to make that happen. *Anything.*'

By now I had cottoned on to what she meant. 'Um, okay, thanks for that,' I stammered. 'You can get away from me now, please.'

There were plenty of tedious aspects to teaching as well. Marking exam papers and dealing with special consideration for students that missed deadlines were top of the list. These were important jobs, don't get me wrong, but not what I set out to spend my time doing. I definitely appreciated the contract and I put in my maximum possible effort but it felt like treading water. I needed to be moving forward, even if it was slowly. Less than half of my time was devoted to research. So I had to be efficient and strategic with my time. I focused on finishing up a few projects and getting prepared for Cambridge.

After Christmas, we packed up our bags and prepared to fly to London. Sydney to London takes about twenty hours of flying time and butterflies did somersaults in my stomach the entire trip. Rachel had taken long service leave and leave without pay from her school psychologist role, and the girls had left their friends behind. The laboratory I would be joining run by Chris Dobson was one of the leading laboratories in the field of protein aggregation. I didn't have a research position to return home to, so the pressure was on to make this count.

There was a lot riding on this stay. The people judging my next funding application would have high expectations.

Our temporary home was a short stroll from the Chemistry Department. Next door to the Chemistry Department was Maddy's school, St Alban's, so we walked together every day. I cherished these mornings. I had that ten minutes where it was just Maddy and me and we could chat about anything. We bought Talia a bicycle to commute to school as the only position available was over the train line and a good thirty-minute walk. I jogged alongside her for the first few weeks to make sure she was comfortable with the directions and riding on the road. The house we were renting was an old brick terrace house, with two storeys and an attic. It was older than any colonial building in Australia. It had three bedrooms on the first floor, which looked over the back garden with its small glass conservatory. We were happy there.

If Chris Dobson was a giant in the field, he was a gentle giant. He was a tall man with soft features and silver hair. He spoke quietly and slowly in his Oxbridge accent as if each word was carefully crafted. Even in anger, his voice didn't raise. Chris's success in science had been assured from his undergraduate days when *Nature*, the most prestigious of all the scientific journals, rang his project supervisor to ask if they had a short paper ready to go because they were about to go to print and there was a little space left. Not a bad start. He had a colossal intellect and his memory seemed to capture everything around him and was available for recall. Even when he seemed distracted, he still had almost total recall. He would on occasion seemingly fall asleep during lectures but would then somehow manage to ask appropriately insightful questions during question time. It was his superpower. Chris would become a mentor and dear friend over the next decade. I owe a lot to Chris.

When I showed up to the department it was Janet who took me in. The joke within the group was that Chris wouldn't even know where the laboratory was. The sheer size of the group made the science seem like it was on an industrial scale compared to Mark's group back in Wollongong. Janet, who I had worked with last time I was in Cambridge, was probably one of the most trusted postdoctoral researchers in Chris's laboratory. She was an intelligent, resourceful, efficient woman with a wealth of knowledge. She was a great mentor day to day. Chris was a particularly busy man and we didn't get much of his time. So if you needed to know anything, Janet was the person to speak to. Janet had moved to Cambridge from Canada and married a Brit and they now lived in a village outside of Cambridge. This meant she had to catch a bus to and from work, and this bookending of the day meant that she had to be efficient with the time she had in the current textbook knowledge to frame cutting-edge research is narrow-minded and that in doing so one might fail to recognise exciting paradigm redefining research. It was in these meetings that I would discover that there was a fundamental flaw in the plan I had come over to Cambridge with. Through data presented by a student, it dawned on me that the amyloid-beta was made inside of cells in the brains of the flies and I had made flies with the chaperone outside of cells in fluids. The experiment was redundant. The two things that I wanted to study would never meet each other. I could sense that all my efforts would be for naught and that I was squandering my opportunity. I needed something else to make the trip worthwhile.

In the office next door to ours in the basement was Giorgio, the same Giorgio I had met a few years before at a party on my previous trip. Giorgio was from the island of Sardinia. He was animated and emotional and hilarious. Chris's executive assistant, Karen, called him the Italian stallion. Giorgio and I had continued our discussions during the current stay about possible experiments to test his ideas. After much discussion and just as much coffee, we decided to do it. This would have been straightforward in the labs back in Wollongong but the Dobson group was not set up to do experiments with cells. It took quite a bit of organising and paperwork but, eventually, we got there. Giorgio's idea was that the size of laboratory. Janet made space on a spare desk in the office she shared with Erwin in the basement of the Unilever Building in the Chemistry Department. The only natural light came in through a shaft that substituted for a window on the wall. The desk that I had been given was covered in stacks of books and printed-out papers so I pushed them to one side and repurposed one book tower as a computer stand and got to work.

The main aim of the study that I was funded to do was to make a genetically modified fruit fly (*drosophila melanogaster*) that made the human protein called alpha-2-macroglobulin that I had discovered was an extracellular chaperone in humans. The idea was to cross these flies with those that made human proteins that aggregated outside cells in diseases such as the amyloid-beta protein in Alzheimer's disease or lysozyme in amyloidosis. This part of the work had to be done in the Genetics Department and so while I set up base in Chemistry, I started to go to meetings and did some lab work in Damian Crowther's fruit fly lab along with a group of others from the Dobson lab. I learned a valuable lesson in the meetings in the Genetics Department. I questioned the purpose of some research being done in the lab because it didn't make rational sense given current knowledge of cell biology. But after looking closely at the data, there could be no other conclusion than what they had drawn. It was clear that using our aggregates would determine how toxic they were because the amount of surface area that would contain water-hating or hydrophobic amino acids would be largest in the small mobile aggregates. What we had to do was to take a panel of proteins and while they were aggregating take samples to measure how big the aggregates were, and how hydrophobic and toxic they were to cells grown in the dish.

This research was not getting me closer to understanding MND but it could get me closer to doing my own MND research through the impact of the project. While I knew that we wouldn't continue to follow this work, at the time it was an exciting scientific adventure. The work that I had done up until now was essentially focused on other people's ideas even if I had designed the experiments. This project was a result of the brainstorming that Giorgio and I had done. It was intellectually stimulating. There is a hard-to-describe feeling you get when you are uncovering some fact that has never been seen, described or understood before. The first human to know a thing. It can be exhilarating. In a way, scientists are explorers and the sense of discovery is intertwined with the sense that what we do is important. It is addictive. I imagine in the same way receiving applause would be addictive for performers.

I asked Janet where we could get some proteins for these experiments. She said that I should speak with Benne. My mind immediately went back to that night at the Free Press and the red wine. Janet said amyloid-beta was hard to work with and that we should think about getting Benne involved. So, Giorgio and I organised a meeting with Benne. She was a PhD student in Chris's group and was supervised by Leila Luheshi and Damian Crowther from Genetics. Benne was a motivated and determined student. Her family came from the foothills of the alps in the north of Italy. She listened to our idea and agreed that it sounded like a great idea and went on to explain how to work with amyloid-beta. Giorgio looked at me and I knew what he was thinking. We asked Benne if she would like to help us with this little project. She agreed. We also brought Janet in on the team.

The four of us made a great team. It was an exciting few months. We ran between instruments as we collected the data. Giorgio offered to help. Benne laughed at the prospect of Giorgio wielding a pipette and banned him from the lab. Giorgio was a theoretician and did his experiments on his computer and Benne didn't want him to get in the way. Giorgio and I would eventually joke that we had created a monster. At the beginning of this little project, we were directing Benne to do particular experiments, but by the end she was telling us what to do.

Once we had put the manuscript together we sent it off to Chris. He scribbled corrections all over the printed document. Likely in a car on the way to the airport or on a plane on the way to a conference. His scrawled notes always covered the entire page. Occasionally words would need a translation from the scribbled scratchings and we would take the page around to others and take a survey on the identity of the word. Eventually, I would become an expert translator.

We sent the manuscript to *Nature Chemical Biology* only to have them tell us that they were already reviewing a similar manuscript. Only the most seemingly important scientific papers are accepted for publication in the *Nature* journals, and publishing in these journals can make or break careers due to their reputation. So it was crushing that someone had beaten us to the punch. We found out that Chris was also an author on the other paper and that stung. Chris has always been supportive so I didn't understand why he hadn't mentioned it to us. After discussion with a few people, it was clear that Chris's group operated in a survival-of-the-fittest framework. At some stage, before my time, there was a structure in the lab and senior postdocs managed a team and projects were distinct. Now it appeared that there was little to no structure and projects sometimes overlapped. I presume that the competition within the group ensured that work got done in a timely manner.

The survival-of-the-fittest style of supervision didn't always produce great work. Occasionally it resulted in power struggles and a breakdown in collegiality. I heard stories of experimental sabotage in the fly lab where people had changed labels on tubes so that experiments would mysteriously not work. There were also struggles between up-and-coming leaders about who owned what project and what students that were so fierce that certain people had to go on stress leave. From my vantage point, there was enough competition between different labs and universities without having such ruthless competition between people in the same group. I honestly think that the measures of success that the scientific community uses has to take some of the blame, as does the fact that there is only funding for the top fifteen per cent of scientists.

***

Our family used our proximity to Europe as a springboard for travel. It has always been something that we have loved to do as a family. We spent Easter in Spain. We met up with friends in Edinburgh and Amsterdam. We also soaked up some sun in Dubrovnik, Positano and Santorini. We loved exploring new places and trying new foods, even though sometimes it didn't work out the way we thought. Like the fried eggplant that Rachel ordered in Granada, that was no more or no less than the name of the dish, and when I ordered a hamburger in Edinburgh only to receive two ham patties deep-fried. We found travelling was also a great way to appreciate the culture of other people and nations. Most of all, I felt so lucky to be spending time with the three people I loved the most.

I continued to write more applications for funding while I was in Cambridge. My goal, of course, was to get funding for MND research but, at this point, I would accept just staying in science. I knew that the chances were small so I kept my expectations in check. I had also found out that Leila had some plasmid DNA for making SOD1 protein, the gene responsible for MND in our family, and she had agreed to share them with me. With these samples, I had the beginnings of my MND research.

One morning I received an email to say that my fellowship application to MND Research Australia had been successful. I read the words over and over several times to make sure that I was reading the email correctly. It still said 'your application has been successful'. It is hard to describe the feeling of achieving a goal that has been ten years in the making and was attached to so much grief and pain. It was a reward for ten years of hard work and all the struggles and literal tears. The reward itself was that I got to start research into the causes of MND. It felt like the culmination of all my focus and energy but, in reality, it was just the beginning.

The work I was funded for was closely related to the work I had been doing over the last six years. I would focus on outside the cell. It was well established that SOD1 spent its entire life inside neurons; however, some work from a young, up-and-coming researcher from Melbourne showed that it could be secreted out of the cell. Brad Turner published this work in 2005. (Brad is a very dedicated MND researcher with whom I get along very well. I feel that we think along similar lines – that our brains work in similar ways. After a conversation with Brad, I always find out two things. First is a catch-up on all the recent papers. He has a photographic memory. Second, we talk about our recent work and many times we have thought similar things and sometimes done similar experiments.)

In the years since 2005, Stan Appel's team had found that if the immune cells of the brain, called microglia, find the mutant form of the SOD1 protein outside cells in the fluid bathing the cells of the brain, they activate a process that is generally reserved for pathogen invaders. Stan thought that this overreaction could result in the accidental death of motor neurons. I wondered if protein aggregates would make the brain's immune system act in the same way as the mutant SOD1 protein before it aggregates. It was, I thought, a natural fit for me to venture out of the work I had been doing with Mark Wilson and into MND research, while remaining at the University of Wollongong. In my first independent research project, I put my first student onto it – she would eventually find that the aggregated form of SOD1 is a more potent activator than the non-aggregated form. It was my first real contribution to the field and a moment to savour after all these years.

DREAM JOURNAL
17 SEPTEMBER 2008

The dream takes place in a kind of WWI-type situation: old weapons, uniforms. It starts with fighting (machine guns and the like, trenches etc) — so much graphic detail, blood, wounds. My troops are decimated and I am left under a pile of bodies. I hear the troops from the other side coming so I hide. The dream then takes the normal run/hide scenario through beautiful golden fields with green mountains in the background. I have to hide below the grass line. Tanks, soldiers go past. I have to kill to stay alive in this dream, though after I kill, the landscape changes. I am hiding in the dark, vegetation-less caves and under houses (dirt, rocks), underground in shadows having to kill the people that find me, always moving on.

Chapter Twelve

Prions

The message was passed to Michael Alpers. Kigea was dead. He knew that what came next was going to be difficult, but it had to be done. It would be nothing compared to what Kigea had endured over the past six months. Kigea had died of a disease known to the Fore people as kuru. The people of the Fore tribe lived in the remote, dense and mountainous jungle of Papua New Guinea. In the 1950s they lived a lifestyle that was seemingly untouched by Western civilisation. Their villages consisted of small, cleared hilltops with groups of circular houses made from woven grasses and palms surrounded by thick jungle that always seemed poised to reclaim the hilltop as soon as the humans were no longer using it. The Fore's territory was dotted with such villages.

Michael Alpers was a young Australian physician who was part of the research team that, during the 1960s, was trying to understand what kuru was and why it was killing so many of the Fore people but not people from other tribes. Today he was going to take some brain samples from Kigea to test whether kuru was infectious. Understanding how people were getting kuru might help prevent cases. Prevention, it seemed, was likely to be the only way to save lives given that the prognosis was invariably death within several months. To test if kuru could be transmitted, they would inject some of the collected brain material into the brains of the closest species to our own, chimpanzees.

Within half an hour of Kigea's death, Michael arrived at the house to scenes of an all-consuming, overpowering grief. Despite the knowledge of what was to come with a diagnosis of kuru, and the fact that she had now escaped the torture that she had endured during the horrendous end stages of the disease when she was unable to move, speak or eat, and was in much pain, the outpouring of grief from her family was still overwhelming. She was only eleven years old, after all. The shouting, wailing and crying did not make the autopsy any easier. So it was that among the grief and with Kigea's uncle holding her up in position, Michael began. He shut out the commotion around him and he tried not to look at her features lest he think about the little girl that he met six months ago when she was a little unsteady on her feet and shyly hiding behind her uncle's leg. Michael quickly retrieved the samples his team would need and after putting everything back in place with neat suturing he gave everybody a hug and left. He departed the jungle for Washington, where medical researcher Carleton Gajdusek was waiting.

Transmission experiments had been done before using kuru brain samples without any hint of infectivity even after six months. This time they were prepared to wait for several years because while no human pathogen that had ever been studied had an incubation period longer than a few weeks, there was a disease in sheep known as scrapie or the trembling disease, which had been found to have incubation periods that were counted in years. The similarities between the trembling disease and kuru were astonishing, so it was worth a shot. If these experiments worked, they would have discovered a totally new type of brain disease. Of particular significance was the fact that no degenerative brain disease had ever been shown to be transmissible between humans.

While they waited for the results of the experiment, Michael focused on epidemiological research looking for clues as to how kuru might be spreading. What he found was astonishing. 'I remember coming into the lab and then suddenly it sprung out at me,' Michael later said in an interview. 'My goodness. This is a major change.' Kuru had seemingly vanished in very young patients. No child born after 1960 had been diagnosed with kuru. The implication of this was that the transmission had been stopped. There was a range of things that had changed for the Fore people in 1960 as new laws under the Australian administration resulted in the eradication of many traditional practices. The most likely cause of the drop in transmission was the halting of the consumption of human meat. So, if kuru was transmissible then the most likely way it was being transmitted was the consumption of the dead during the mortuary feasts, which, in essence, were religious practices to free the spirit of dead loved ones from their earthly body.

Two years after Michael had taken samples of Kigea's brain it was obvious that it was possible to transmit the disease to chimps. So, researchers looked closely at the brain material hoping to find a virus. But no matter how hard Carleton Gajdusek searched he could not find any evidence of a virus. He couldn't even find an immune response in people with kuru that would be expected with any other known virus. However, the material seemed to respond to treatment that would destroy protein molecules, suggesting that the transmissible agent either depended on or was composed of protein. While much of the initial transmission work presumed that a virus was the transmission agent, neurologist Stanley Prusiner was developing an idea that misfolded proteins could act in a manner that mimics infection. He called these proteins prions. His work suggested that instead of a virus replicating in the brain tissue being responsible for the transmission, proteins were converting to a disease-causing shape, then coaxing others into the same shape. This was such a huge departure from the way we understood diseases to transfer from one person to the next that Prusiner took decades to convince people that it was indeed a protein that was responsible for the transmissibility and that the shape of the prion protein was the information passed from one molecule to the next. Both Carleton Gajdusek and Stanley Prusiner would be awarded Nobel Prizes for their work. Famously the mad cow disease outbreak in the UK and subsequent transfer to humans where it was known as new variant Creutzfeldt-Jakob disease (CJD) was caused by prion protein.

Off the back of the new understanding that it was possible for neurodegenerative diseases to be transmitted, there was a flurry of experiments to test if MND could be transmitted from human to primate brains. A Russian laboratory reported that they had transmitted MND to primates from brain material taken from MND patients. Gajdusek and his team had failed to transmit MND to primates, so the Russian results caused something of a sensation. However, the field came together to retest the Russian samples and eventually they concluded that the Russian claims had been incorrect. There had been no real transmission of MND. The death of the monkeys was more likely to be caused by a cage infection with some other unrelated virus.

After reviewing all their experiments, Gajdusek and his team reported that two 'atypical cases' of MND with dementia successfully transmitted a neurodegenerative condition out of thirty-three attempts, leaving the door open to the possibility that some forms of MND could be transmitted. It is important to note here that failure of transmission does not necessarily exclude the possibility of prion or prion-like disease. It may just have meant that in most tests the right conditions to permit transmission had not been found or that the transmission agent in MND could not efficiently jump the species barrier.

It was almost three decades later that I started thinking about the role transmissibility might play in MND. At the time, nothing more had been added to the field. The applicability of the concept of the prion model of transmission to other neurodegenerative disorders had become more nuanced in the first decade of the twenty-first century. In conditions such as Parkinson's disease and Huntington's disease, rather than thinking about transmission in terms of from one person to another, it was thought that a transmission of a protein shape from one neuron to the next might explain the propagation of the disease through the nervous system. So, given this new way of thinking and the elegant work of neurologist John Ravits showing that MND starts in a focal point and spreads out from that point, I started working seriously on the problem in 2010.

It seemed to me that understanding if protein shape could be responsible for the orderly progression of MND would provide potential drug targets. If I wanted to understand more though, I would need funding and a team. I wouldn't be able to do it on my own. Coming up with ideas is one thing, but doing all the lab work required for such an ambitious project is another thing entirely. I would need a piece of preliminary evidence to convince grant panels that this would be a mechanism of disease progression worthy of study. I needed to show that aggregates could get inside cells and that once inside they could start to coerce the developing protein to join the aggregate rather than fold properly.

I applied for a National Health and Medical Research Council (NHMRC) project grant to allow me to really dig into these ideas. After submitting my proposal in March 2010, the outcome would be announced in October. During October I think that I refreshed my email more times than I had in my entire life. My fingernails were chewed until there was nothing left to chew. To the surprise of everyone, including myself, I got the grant. Here I was just two years after graduating with my PhD and I had my own NHMRC funding. Some researchers at the university had applied year after year without success. This was kind of a big deal and now that I had it, I found myself wondering if I could do it. By this point I couldn't turn back; this was really happening. I looked back to the list of goals that I had made in undergraduate class. I had methodically ticked off each step. Slowly but surely. Step by step. Now here I was standing on the mountaintop. Time to set new goals. Time to set my sights on the moon.

I felt I was gaining momentum and that nothing could stand in my way. I felt that somehow everything would just fall into place. I started to actually believe, for the first time, that I may actually be able to make a difference. After receiving the grant, one professor from the department stopped me in the hall to offer me a backhanded congratulations: 'Congratulations, but that is your free one used up. Now the test will be if you can continue to get funding.' I didn't care what anyone thought; I would be doing what I had set out to do. I would be shining a light on some of the shadows of MND. I would be doing research that no one else was doing. This work would be the first time that the prion-like hypothesis would be tested in MND. The idea was to make protein aggregates from the protein that we had generated and see if cells would take them up and then see if those aggregates could seed further aggregate formation in the cell. If this held true then we might have found an explanation for the pattern of motor neuron loss in MND.

While my own research was taking off, I also wanted to hear the very latest MND research from the researchers themselves. I found that during lectures people would, with clarity, explain how they came to do certain experiments and how they came to certain conclusions, much more clearly than can be written in a paper. I vowed to try to attend as many MND/ALS symposia as possible. I thought that it would be worth the trip even if I heard just one nugget of information that I could add to my understanding of MND.

I flew to Orlando in December 2010 just after I had been funded to do the first research on the prion-like hypothesis applied to MND. So I was particularly interested in a talk by a neurologist from the University of British Columbia in Canada. Neil Cashman was a softly spoken but dogmatic neuroscientist. He was a short figure with white hair and a wellkept beard and he was wearing a suit. The person chairing this particular session mentioned that Neil would not be able to answer any questions today as he had to leave immediately to catch a flight. Beside the stage, his suitcase sat at the ready, parked in anticipation like a getaway car. As Neil spoke, I realised more and more that my idea wasn't as unique as I thought. I knew that there was no way that I would be able to compete with this professor's team. As he finished his talk and he kept his promise of not hanging around to answer questions, I thought, *I wish that I had the chance to talk with him.* I don't know what gave me the courage to get up out of my chair but I found myself running after Neil to catch him before he got in a cab and drove away. I caught him and blurted out, 'I really liked your talk – have you got one minute to talk?' He said that we could talk as we walked. I thanked him. He seemed like a nice guy. I explained that I had been working with Chris Dobson and that I had just been awarded three years of funding to work on the ideas he had just finished talking about. This stopped him in his tracks. Now I had his full attention. We chatted briefly as he listened intently. He told me to email him and there might be potential to work together. This was the moment that made my trip to Orlando worthwhile.

One of the first things that I learned about research was how science measures impact or innovation. Scientists need a measure for these things so that they might judge which science gets in the most prestigious journals like *Nature* or *Science*, and judge their fellow scientists in order to decide if they should be funded. One event, in particular, provided a masterclass in how science works. One brilliant scientist from a prestigious American university – let's call him Steve – has an uncanny knack for publishing cutting-edge science. Many scientists have a strong conviction that their view of the field is correct and it takes a lot to change their mind, if it is at all possible. Others toil on a particular area, building brick by brick a body of work so that it all stands together, strong and recognisable as one larger contribution to the field. This man is different. He is a populist, a scientist who changes his direction to be the first to capitalise on a particular trend or popular idea, and he is good at it. I met him at a conference on Heron Island on the Great Barrier Reef. Heron Island is a small coral island that has one resort and thousands of birds called noddies that give the island a pungent odour that cannot be escaped, and a constant honking so that the island sounds like a busy metropolis. The island is also home to the egrets for which the island is incorrectly named. I had given a presentation on the work I had been doing with Neil Cashman.

Steve showed himself to be a natural and charismatic presenter. He guided the audience through his work with ease and kept everyone engaged with comedic moments. His performance lulled you into the idea that he was being open, whereas I felt he revealed just enough to give this impression and not enough to truly understand exactly what he had found.

Three months after the Heron Island conference, he published a review article on the prion topic in the top journal in cell and molecular biology called *Cell*. Steve had no interest in this area before or after this paper; he was just taking advantage of a field about to take off. You might wonder why someone publishing in a particular area I was working on would raise emotions. After all, the more people contributing to MND research would mean much-needed discoveries were made faster. The problem is that in order to keep researching you need funding and to get the funding you need to show that you are a research innovator and a research leader. I made a mental note to be more guarded and to only work with good people.

In terms of working with good people, Neil Cashman is one of the best. Neil has been a great person to work with. Since the time I first met Neil as he made a dash to his taxi, I have found him to be a kind and generous man who has always found time to talk. I have had some very personal and emotional conversations with him during tough times. I am lucky enough to call him a friend.

Neil has worked on several neurodegenerative diseases over his career, including the prion disorders. This broad study obviously influenced his thinking about MND. Neil had a strong conviction that small amounts of aggregate SOD1 protein could speed up the process and could be transmitted from one cell to another. That is, act in a manner that mimics the prion protein, although there was never a suggestion that it was contagious or could be transmissible between humans. Conceptually, the idea was that the small amount of misfolded and aggregated protein can coax the normal form of the protein to change shape and join the aggregated material, eventually causing most of a cell's protein to become misshapen. This is the protein equivalent of a zombie apocalypse. The misfolded protein is like a zombie in that a zombie changes regular humans into zombies when they attack, usually eating their brain in the process. Ironically, kuru was transmitted to family members through the eating of a dead relative's brain out of respect or tribute. This zombie protein idea is useful when thinking about how a very small number of molecules can result in a change across the entire population. Once a molecule has changed its neighbours, which in turn transform their neighbours, the process grows exponentially, resulting in a misfolding apocalypse. Importantly, Neil was able to find the same altered form of the protein in human tissue as we saw in the test tube and we were able to publish our work in the *Proceedings of the National Academy of Sciences* (PNAS) in 2014.

One experiment I think that really showed that misfolded protein could indeed result in the apparent spread of MND through the nervous system was one we conducted in collaboration with Dr Jake Ayres from the University of Florida. He had discovered that extracts from the spinal cord of mice that had MND symptoms from the human mutant SOD1 could cause MND in other mice that did not have MND. He injected the material into mice that were engineered to get MND but did not. So it took the injection of spinal cord extract to trigger the disease. What we were able to show was that our purified protein could trigger the same disease as the spinal cord material, which confirmed our hypothesis that misfolded protein could indeed cause the spread of the disease through the nervous system.

I felt we were getting closer.

DREAM JOURNAL
16 OCTOBER 2012

The dream starts: I am looking for something. I have found out too much. Masked man comes to where I am hiding with guns. I have to fight off the men with a machine gun I find. Taking refuge behind anything I can. People around won't help me. Have to fight them on my own. A big battle ensues. I think I am going to die.

Chapter Thirteen

A Fantastical Submarine World

Auguste sat on the edge of the bed, her head hung low with a look that one could only describe as helpless. The room contained several cast-iron beds lined up on one side of the room with sheets tucked so tightly as if to stop patients from escaping. She was a 51-year-old woman with a long, expressionless face that made her look much older, a face that told a story about the kind of life she had led in the second half of the nineteenth century in Hamburg. Here, in the psychiatric hospital, she was attended to by Dr Alois Alzheimer. Alois was a very passionate neurologist, with a round face, a handlebar moustache and spectacles chained to the jacket of his three-piece suit.

'What is your name?' he asked her.
'Auguste,' she replied.
'And your husband's name?'
'Auguste, I think.'

Dr Alzheimer then asked Auguste to write Mrs Auguste Dieter in his notebook. She wrote Mrs but then seemed to forget what she was writing and needed prompting.

Auguste had been brought to this facility because without warning she had had fits of jealousy and started to forget things. She was able to tell the doctors what objects were such as a pen, but would soon forget what she had been asked to write with the pen. Alzheimer was convinced that psychiatric disorders must have a physical origin in the brain and was hoping to be able to prove such a link. On this day, he took extensive case notes and, five years later, after Auguste succumbed to her condition, he was able to dissect her brain. What he found was an obvious shrinking of the brain and the presence of lesions that we now know as plaques and tangles. When he presented these findings, he proposed that the plaques and tangles were responsible for her clinical symptoms.

We now know that the plaques and tangles are protein deposits and that many disease states are associated with similar abnormal protein deposits comprised of aggregated protein, including an insoluble fibrillar aggregate known as amyloid. The field of protein aggregation or fibril formation really began in the mid-1980s with the discovery of the main component of amyloid plaques from Alzheimer's-disease brains. Soon after the discovery of the amyloid-beta protein by Colin Masters, Dennis Selkoe independently discovered that amyloid-beta could spontaneously aggregate into rope-like fibrils similar to those found in the brains of people with Alzheimer's disease. These studies were the birth of the thinking that these protein aggregates might be responsible for the death of neurons in the brains of people with a range of neurodegenerative diseases.

The protein deposits are only found in the brains of people with a neurological disorder, so the question of how a normally soluble and folded protein ends up in these deposits has been one of particular interest since the mid-eighties. The way a protein takes a particular shape or fold (as I mentioned in the previous chapter) is essential to living organisms because it provides the functional machinery for the genetic blueprint from which it is made. However, correct protein folding is not necessarily assured. With millions of protein molecules per cell, the critical question becomes how does the cell keep all those molecules from clustering together and aggregating?

Inside each of the thirty trillion cells that make up the human body is a fantastical submarine world. If you could peek inside it would be like watching the tumultuous hustle and bustle of a busy, crowded coral reef. There are thousands upon thousands of different proteins floating around, jiggling like jelly on a plate, in the briny cellular sea. Some are walking along the solid skeleton that frames the cell. One foot in front of the other, carrying sacks filled with cargo. Others are turning like a turbine to generate energy, while still others protrude from the large immovable components of the cell, like barnacles on a rock. There are many, many copies of each protein, like tiny armies dutifully carrying out their particular job. All in all, there are millions and millions of protein molecules in each and every cell in your body. In fact, there are so many individual protein molecules that by some estimates there are more protein molecules in an average-sized human than there are stars in the universe or grains of sand on all the beaches on Earth.

The mind-boggling number of protein molecules in the human body is made all the more impressive when you consider that this is just one snapshot in time, and that half of these protein molecules will be removed from circulation in forty-eight hours and replaced by freshly made versions of themselves. I don't think that we have a word for the staggering number of protein molecules that exist in a human over an entire lifetime, and even if we did there would be no adequate way for me to describe it to you. There would certainly not be anything to compare it to. Let's just agree that it is a very, very large number of protein molecules. Unfathomably large.

The human body is around thirty per cent protein, which means that in a fifty-kilogram human every forty-eight hours 7.5 kilograms of protein is destroyed and made again. It is vital to make sure all the proteins are maintained in good working order, even if that means replacing aged proteins. Life absolutely depends on it. It is a huge task. That is around 1,000,000,000,000,000,000,000 individual protein molecules that have to be made every two days. A staggering feat of engineering. And typically speaking, when this occurs in a healthy individual, the large majority of the protein molecules end up folded into the correct shape. Proteins don't only accumulate in misfolded forms and create deposits just in young healthy people. About ten per cent of all proteins made have a job that is to ensure that the right protein is made at the right time, right place and in the right number. This protein quality control system is in charge of the billions of trillions of proteins made and disposed of over your entire life.

After the critical discovery of the link between the misfolded proteins with various neurodegenerative diseases, there was a surge of research into the biochemical description of protein quality control – the logic being that there must be a breakdown in the quality control system if misfolded proteins escape its watchful eye only after a person has aged. The protein misfolding field studied a narrow view of the mechanisms in place to ensure that a given protein could transition from a linear chain of amino acids to a fully folded and functional protein without becoming part of an insoluble aggregate. The main players in the orchestra of machinery that ensured that a protein stayed in its functional form were the chaperones, the type of protein I studied in my PhD that help fold a protein, and the protein degradation or recycling system to remove proteins that are unable to fold. The research field was squarely focused on how a cell normally prevented protein aggregation, given that its apparent importance to conditions ranging from some form of cancers, diabetes and a host of neurodegenerative diseases were associated with deposits of misfolded and aggregated proteins.

During the first decade of this century, it was becoming clear that this view was an inadequate oversimplification. The first clue that a more holistic understanding was required came in 2004 when Ellen Nollen and Rick Morimoto teamed up to study the genes that modified the amount of protein aggregation in laboratory worms. Lab worms are similar to lab rats in that they are well used to study the basic principles of life, only the worms are not as complicated so it is easier to understand what is happening. Nollen and Morimoto silenced each of the worm genes in turn and then looked at the worm to see if it increased or decreased protein aggregation. What they found was that the genes that modified aggregation fell into a handful of specific categories. The categories that stood out from the data were in simple terms: i) making a protein, ii) recycling of protein molecules, and iii) moving a protein throughout the cell. This study changed the way protein aggregation was thought about and it broadened the scope of the known levers that a cell could pull to affect the process of protein aggregation.

The ideas that were percolating in a range of laboratories across the globe were crystallised by Rick Morimoto, Andrew Dillin, Jeff Kelly and Bill Balch in 2008. They introduced a new concept to the protein misfolding field that centred on the cellular maintenance of *all* of a cell's protein molecules, moving away from thinking solely about disease-associated proteins. They called this new concept protein homeostasis or its portmanteau proteostasis. It was a huge shift in the way we think about the life and times of proteins in the cell. It may have been the biggest leap forward since Crick's paper on protein synthesis in 1958.

When I started to think about MND through the lens of proteostasis, the thing that stood out to me was that the genetic mutations that had been found to be associated with MND fit nicely into the categories that Rick Morimoto had identified as affecting protein aggregation. So I began to think about what that might mean. And I kept thinking about this over the next decade. The first thing that I did with this concept that was continuing to grow and evolve inside my mind was to apply for funding to research the topic further. I was lucky enough to be successful in my application to the Australian Research Council and receive a fellowship in 2012. Only twelve per cent of all applications that year were funded across all areas of research.

I tried to explain these ideas to a well-respected neurologist while I was at the ALS MND Symposium in Chicago in December 2012. He listened intently and, after a thoughtful pause, he said, 'That can't be right because it is too complicated. The answer will be simple and elegant.' I didn't bother trying to further explain the elegance of the hypothesis. I knew that I would have to collect evidence so that these ideas would hold true.

Around the same time that I had this conversation, our team held our own conference focused on the concept of proteostasis. Having the leading scholars in Wollongong was the main reason for holding the meeting in our hometown. The experience of hosting the likes of Chris Dobson, Rick Morimoto and Ulrich Hartl in 2014 was priceless for our students. As it turned out, the most valuable interaction for me wasn't with the big-name professors but a student. Prajwal Ciryam was a PhD student who was splitting his time between Chicago and Cambridge under the tutelage of Rick Morimoto, Chris Dobson and Michele Vendruscolo. He was a very confident and charismatic speaker for someone so early in his career. He won our student speaker prize unanimously. Prajwal was using existing data sets to study the cumulative risk of aggregation in humans. Apparently, he had been politely told to stay away from the lab in his first few weeks in Cambridge after his laboratory skills were found lacking. That was probably the best thing that could have happened to him because he excelled at the theoretical side of things.

Around this time I had been thinking about how a misfolded protein might be related to toxicity in motor neurons. With the existing knowledge, it was and still is impossible to say for certain if the aggregate causes cell dysfunction or if it is a result of cellular dysfunction. Perhaps both are true. Regardless, the fact that they exist at all is an indication that proteostasis is out of balance. This is probably the least understood aspect of the deposits. One thought has been that the deposit is a sign that the system in charge of maintaining protein quality control has been overwhelmed. I like to think of this overwhelmed cell like a fire service in a town that has a strong and continuous extra blaze to fight. What this would likely mean for the community protected by that fire service is that the service is so distracted with that one fire that other houses might be more likely to end up with more damage than they would have otherwise had. The implication then is that because of the system overload any number of other unrelated proteins might be compromised.

Another way that the deposits may be detrimental to cells is the possibility that proteins that are sucked into the deposits may no longer be available to do their normal job in the cell. It was understood that there were a number of proteins that were found in the deposits but we really didn't know the full extent. To find evidence that protein homeostasis has been disturbed in general I started collating a list of proteins that are found in deposits. These proteins are the equivalent of the extra houses that get burned because the fire service gets stretched too thin. It took months of checking through published work to find all that was currently known about which proteins are in the deposits. I didn't know what I was going to do with the list until I saw Prajwal's talk.

Prajwal thought that the proteins found in deposits across a range of neurodegenerative diseases were there because they were proteins at risk. (Continuing the fire-service analogy, they are the proteins that had the most flammable material so most likely to catch fire.) He identified the risk as a phenomenon known as supersaturation. Simply it means that the risk of a protein being found in a deposit is related to the level of a particular protein. If it is higher than you would normally expect then we would say that it is supersaturated.

The most spectacular example of supersaturation at work is the making of snowflakes. Water molecules accumulate in the atmosphere and if sufficiently cold and if the water molecules become so concentrated that there are more squeezed into a volume of air than would normally be found, they will crystallise into solid snowflakes. The key being the change in the water molecules from one state to another – from mobile individual water molecules floating around on their own to a solid crystal with molecules bound up in the solid state. Precisely the same thing occurs with proteins. That is, if a protein has more molecules floating around than might normally be expected, it is at risk of becoming part of a solid deposit.

I gave Prajwal the list I'd collated of proteins found in deposits and, using his numbers to perform the calculation, he found that the average supersaturation for my list was higher than the average of all the remaining proteins in a cell. It would take another five years of meetings in various cafés around the world and over Skype, and refinement of the results before we would publish the manuscript on our findings. What we had found was that the proteins known to be in deposits were indeed some of the most at-risk proteins in the cell. To use the fire analogy, they were the houses most at risk of catching fire once the fire service was distracted, meaning they were the first to get damaged when the fire service was overwhelmed. The next question we had to answer was what was distracting the fire service in the first place.

We had been studying the SOD1 protein in which there are many mutations that are associated with MND. What was known from studying people with these mutations was that different mutations resulted in different outcomes. Some mutations resulted in rapidly progressive disease and other mutations were known to result in slow-progressing disease with survival predicted of over ten years. Of course, these are averages and there can be variation within a family. Within our family we had some people live only a matter of months after diagnosis while others lived for almost a decade.

A student in my laboratory, Luke McAlary, had shown that there was a strong correlation between how severe a mutation was and how much it unfolded and aggregated in the laboratory. This was our clue that in the case of families with mutated SOD1, the SOD1 protein was chronically misfolded and this was likely the continuous fire that distracted protein quality control elements away from their normal job.

The commitment and drive of my team in the lab was growing, as we continued to make further inroads into understanding the causes and expression of MND. With these advances came confidence in the capacity for their own work to make a difference.

DREAM JOURNAL: 29 JANUARY 2014

There is a flood coming – everything I do is in order to get my family away from the flood. Our house was going to be swept away. It was a flood of biblical proportions. I could not seem to get everyone together to escape. And how were we going to escape with everyone else doing the same?

We had to make it to the top of the escarpment; only there would we be safe. We set off – there was so much water that it was oozing from every hill, patch of grass or tree. Soon we would be swallowed up by the rising swells and even the land was turning to a liquidy beast. At every turn, water turned us back. It was as if we would never make it above the flood.

Chapter Fourteen

Hyperexcitability and Darkness

One day at the beginning of 2015, I was getting ready for work. The monotonous routine that I had honed over the years gave me a kind of comfort. Getting the girls ready for their day kept me in touch with their lives as they got older. A shower, quick breakfast and brushing of my teeth, a cheese sandwich for me and lunch for the kids then I was on my way. This particular and most ordinary morning, as I raised my arm to brush my teeth, it wouldn't go all the way up.

I tried again.

Still, my toothbrush didn't make it to my mouth.

My heart started to beat faster and I could feel the rhythm of it in my head. Now I was getting concerned. I shook my shoulder and arm around as if there were something weighing it down when I knew perfectly well there was not.

One last try.

Okay, it wasn't going to happen. The floor of the bathroom swayed beneath my feet and perspiration started to form beads on my forehead. There was no pain in the shoulder, it just wasn't working. This was the worst combination of symptoms, of words to speak. So I said nothing. I didn't have time for this. I brushed my teeth with my left arm and I went to work. I couldn't shake the feeling that this was MND. I tried to calm down by telling myself that in the past I had thought that a twitch here or there or a muscle not doing what it was told was MND. I told myself I was fine.

    I remember with great clarity the day, many years earlier in 2001, that I first had a muscle twitch. It was a small flicker in my left calf muscle. I was waiting for Talia to come out of school and I just stood and watched the twitch flicker on and off for about ten minutes. Such a small thing but it induced some primitive fear response like Pavlov's dog. Doctors call these twitches fasciculations. The twitches are involuntary muscle contractions and relaxations. I think of it like trying to start a car with a flat battery. It's as if the muscle tries to start but doesn't make a full muscle movement. It is sometimes associated with MND but muscle twitching is something that a lot of people experience. Twitching in the eyelid muscles is probably the most common. Perhaps you have experienced this yourself? My cousin Ashley had described it as feeling like worms were moving around under his skin. The whole family knew about the twitches and the flickering of muscles, and whether they were part of MND or not was something that would haunt us all.

Thinking that you have an untreatable, unrelenting and always fatal disease is a special kind of torture. Not only for me but also for those who love and rely on me. So, I generally chose to keep these thoughts and fears to myself. But sometimes it was unavoidable. This was one of those times. I had to tell Rachel.

I called our neurologist, Dom Rowe, and said I needed an urgent appointment. He squeezed me in. When I finally got to see him, we chit-chatted for a bit as was our custom before I told him about the weakness and restriction in my shoulder. His expression tightened and the joviality of our earlier conversation turned to something steely and business-like. *This is bad news*, I thought. My heart skipped a beat, then began to gallop. The possibility of having MND was becoming more and more a reality. He did a physical exam, leaving the bad shoulder for last, as if perhaps giving it more time would help it improve.

When I stuck my left elbow out to the side Dom pulled down on it, but the strength of the shoulder prevailed. It was like a strange arm wrestle. He asked me to do the same with the right shoulder. This time he managed to pull it all the way back down. Something was really wrong. We sat down to talk about what the possibilities were for what he was seeing. We didn't discuss MND but it remained the elephant in the room, and the room wasn't that big.

He asked if I had damaged the shoulder. I had. Four weeks prior I was mountain biking with some mates and I had crashed and landed on my right shoulder. It was sore for a couple of weeks. Dom said that there was a possibility that the symptoms could be a result of tendon damage. So he sent me for an MRI and said, 'Let's look at each other in a few weeks.'

The time between appointments was rough. Waiting for that kind of life-or-death news can send a person into an emotional tailspin. Finding space inside your mind to think about anything else is almost impossible. It helped that the kids and my lab members were oblivious to my struggle so they treated me as if there was nothing wrong and demanded my time and attention as was the norm. Regardless, my thoughts darkened and the nightmares of being chased by an unknown figure returned.

Rachel and I returned to Dom's office with the worst outcome in both our minds but we don't speak it out loud lest it gives the thoughts life. The walk from the waiting room to Dom's office felt longer than usual, like walking to the courtroom to hear your sentence. My very own bridge of sighs.

'First things first. Let's talk about the MRI results. There is no obvious structural damage,' said Dom.

I knew that this was bad news.

It was our alternate diagnosis and that only left one thing. He mentioned that the MRI was not particularly clear because I had moved in the machine. I had moved, I confirmed. Not voluntarily though. The MRI had made my thumb twitch like crazy. Dom said that some people were just more excitable before quickly adding that his wife Sally also had the same issue. Dom and I went through the same dance as we had the last visit. Pull here, push there. Again leaving the bad arm until last. This time when he asked me to push up with the right arm, I won the arm wrestle. He tried harder, but couldn't pull it down. He put his entire body weight on my arm, but still I resisted. Dom did a little jig of excitement on his way back to his desk.

This was not MND. Once you lose mobility of a limb with MND the strength does not return. Not like that. The decline is inexorable.

We left Dom's office a little lighter but exhausted. It felt like I had just got away with murder. On the way back to the car, Rachel finally let the pressure release and she broke down and cried. 'I am okay,' I said. But inside something felt that the clock had started ticking, marking the beginning of the end. I just couldn't shake the feeling and I couldn't stop thinking about something Dom had said. 'Some people are just more excitable than others.'

The fact that motor neurons are hyperexcitable in people with MND had been known for a while. I contributed my body to some early experiments, as a family non-MND control, back when my mother had the disease.

The experiment stimulated the brain and measured output on the right thumb. The stimulation at intervals felt like being whacked on top of the head and some of my family members pulled out because of the discomfort. The results from these types of studies on members of our family would uncover an important fact. The motor neurons of people with MND were hyperexcitable.

Those very innocent words from Dom rattled around and around in my head and I could not escape them. These thoughts were a destructive force unravelling the fabric of my sense of self, thread by thread. It didn't help that for the first time in seven years I had missed out on a fellowship. So, when my contract ended in June 2015, I would not have a position. Only career researchers know what it feels like to submit a funding application in March only to have to wait until November to find out if you still have funding for the next year. On the day of the funding announcements, researchers are paralysed except for the ability to refresh the funding body's webpage hoping to have a future in science next year. The stress is unhealthy and sensible people opt out of the system after a few cycles, meaning science as a whole loses great scientists each year. I had no idea what I would do after June.

My close call with a diagnosis of MND took its toll on me. I knew the statistics and what the prevalence of MND in people carrying a faulty gene meant. It was highly likely that I would not live past the age of fifty. The fact that my plan to shine a light on the darkest shadows of MND may soon come to an end meant that not only did I feel that the candle of my life was burning low but that my way of pushing back was being taken away. People would often say to me that they didn't think that they would be able to work on and think so much about the disease that posed an existential threat to their lives. My response to this was that I had always been able to compartmentalise my research and keep it from the corners of my mind that I reserved for my thoughts on MND and its possible destruction of my life. But now the thoughts of MND taking over were bleeding into every part of my mind and I could not stem the flow. Darkness was clinging to me like a wet shirt and I couldn't shake it off.

Stephen Hawking was once asked by a child what would happen if someone fell into a black hole. He thought about it for a second and replied that they would turn into spaghetti. An answer that thoroughly satisfied the youngster. I had been feeling the immense gravity of the MND black hole moving me faster and faster towards the complete and inescapable darkness. Now that I was on the precipice, time had slowed. Pulling on my being and stretching me out like spaghetti until I thought I would break.

I walked in the shadows of death that year. It followed me everywhere. My thoughts grew increasingly dark and I noticed micro thoughts popping into my head like the whispers of a friend. They would tell me to steer the car into that pole at high speed, or take some of that toxic chemical or step off that balcony. These suggestions were not my own thoughts and I never contemplated taking my own life but the darkness was my constant companion and its whispers were a result of that. The fleeting voices had no place in my rational brain so I managed to ignore their gentle whispers. Once upon a time, after weighing up both sides of the argument, I thought that it would be a reasonable thing to do to end your own life if you had a diagnosis of MND. I thought that going out on your own terms before you were robbed of your independence and dignity was attractive. I was much younger then and my sense of self was tied up with my physicality more than now. And while that decision seemed to me at the time rational and born from logic, it did not take into consideration matters of the heart. The love that tethered me to my girls was not logical but it was strong. I knew that, more than anything, I wanted to live. I had so much to live for, but the darkness kept trying to drag me under.

With the little voices and the shadows that followed me I was racked with anxiety. My stomach churned and my legs were weak. All the time. I took to the bottle. I had a newfound love of red wine. I had been introduced to it in the most romantic of settings. We were staying with friends in their country house in Chianti in the Tuscan hills. They had a bottle from the local vineyard down the road and we had a glass or two over dinner. It was an Italian institution and who was I to argue. It was a very civilised hobby that I used as a cover for self-medication. I started drinking every day. I had only ever drunk alcohol in social settings and was typically restricted to weekends. So this was something new. I would just have a couple of glasses of wine but in the biggest glass I could find. Just enough to relax and take away the unrelenting angst. Sometimes a larger dose would be required.

My aim was not to get drunk. That was counterproductive. Where I once was a happy drunk I was more and more a much darker shade of drunk. One who couldn't cope with large groups and was more melancholy and anxious. I was a walking, breathing contradiction. I wanted to live and experience the world but at the same time I just wanted to curl up into a ball and stay home. I said yes to adventures in 2015. A weekend with Rachel and friends on a boat sailing around the Whitsunday Islands. Yes. A friend's wedding in Sardinia. Yes. An invitation to speak at a conference in Jerusalem. Yes. A conference in Cavtat, Croatia; in Rome; in Brussels. Yes, yes, yes. When I did drink too much, when the cacophony of the voices in the restaurant or conference function reached a crescendo in my mind, I would escape into the cool night air and pace the streets of a foreign city. Occasionally this didn't calm my nerves and I would eventually cry myself to sleep.

Rachel didn't deserve any of this. She had supported every endeavour that I had embarked on, whether it was folly or something more meaningful. She had put her dreams and career on hold and this was supposed to be her time. She had started her own research only last year after many years of wanting to combine her love for nature and in particular dolphins with her interest in psychological well-being. I didn't want to bring my darkness in to my home life. I had to compartmentalise my life. I had been doing it for years, keeping the research I did on MND separate from my life and vice versa. I had become very good at it, but now I introduced a new compartment.

Given that I had been unsuccessful with my fellowship application, I decided that I would re-apply and hope that the university would help out with six months of salary while I waited for the outcome. I realised that there are no guarantees in life but the cycle of grants just to get another short contract seemed particularly cruel. If the university agreed to pay me for another six months, it would surely be my last shot at staying in research doing the work I had spent so many years studying and preparing to do. It was while I was in the early stages of preparing a hopefully improved application that I received the following message.

I am pleased to advise that your application was high on the reserve listing and is now approved for funding.

The NHMRC had given me a second-round offer. I read and reread the email a dozen times before I could believe that I had a fellowship. I didn't even know that the NHMRC had second-round offers. Apparently, the approval of recommendations by the then Minister for Health, for career development fellowships commencing in 2015, included provision for additional offers to be made to replace those not accepted in the initial round.

I should have been excited, but all I felt was a profound sense of relief. It was a four-year fellowship. The longest time that I had ever been given to do work and not have to keep applying for my own salary. This would give me a chance to think about new projects and new ideas. That was what was important. I didn't have time to celebrate. I needed to get on with it.

DREAM JOURNAL:
13 MAY 2015

In this dream, I am locked in a large over-sized house. I have to evade the unknown attackers. I hide under giant-sized furniture such as beds. I do have to fight the attackers, though, with all my might to protect people I have with me. The furniture in the dream reminds me of the furniture in the bedrooms in Nan and Pop Yerbury's house in Young.

I do not give in and allow the unknown attackers to win.

Chapter Fifteen

The Beast Closes In

Despite the tumultuous nature of the previous twelve months, at the beginning of 2016 my career was still on the rise. I had just had my abstract selected for a presentation at the proteostasis conference to be held at Cold Spring Harbor in New York. This was the pre-eminent meeting in the field. I had, I felt, finally been accepted into the upper echelons of my peers. I had come so far since those first small steps I had taken in undergraduate classes fifteen years ago. In the last six years that I had been doing MND research, I had published a string of papers on how the prion hypothesis may explain the progression of MND through the nervous system and I had started to build a reputation in the field of proteostasis. The knowledge we had created had been added, like growth rings, to the ever-growing tree of knowledge of MND. In time, our discoveries will be grown over and built upon but will always be a part of the tree. Nobody can take that away.

It really felt like we were starting to build momentum. I say *we* because without my students and staff I would not have been able to make the same kind of progress. Science really is a team game. I had been invited to give talks at various universities and international conferences. People were starting to take notice. Things were looking up. And although we hadn't illuminated all of the darkness around MND, we had at least started to shine a light on it. We still had much to do but I was growing more and more confident that we could make a real impact. At least I did up until the moment that I flew to New York to attend the conference at Cold Spring Harbor.

That is when my thumb stopped working.

I had a very bad feeling about this one. I thought that I had used up my luck the previous year and there were only so many times that I could dodge the bullet. I told myself at the time that the only issue I had was with my thumb. It was far from being a creeping paralysis. I knew that MND never stopped taking more and more from you, that it was relentless, so while there was no weakness anywhere else in my body, I could try to believe that the problem with my thumb was something else. Anything else would be better.

It was entirely possible that it could be the result of some kind of nerve damage. Something as simple as driving a lot with your elbow resting on the partially rolled-down window can put enough pressure on the nerve as it traverses the elbow to damage the nerve that feeds the thumb. It just goes to show how fragile nerves can be. Even armed with several possible explanations for my thumb not working, I still had an overwhelming sense that the day of the neurology appointment that I subsequently made would mark the divide between my life before and after. I worried it would mark the end of my life as I knew it. More importantly, it would be the end of life as Rachel, Talia and Maddy knew it. The trajectory of the lives of my girls would be irreversibly altered.

Rachel and I once again travelled to see Dom, hoping that he could once more provide some hope that our lives would not be torn apart. The physical examination was the normal dance of push and pull and pull and push. Only after the full-body examination did he focus on my thumb. It had no strength at all. He didn't have to spend much time looking at it. He then used a pin to prick areas of my palm. If the thumb damage was because of nerve damage then both movement and sensation would be affected. The sensation across the palm is felt by two main nerves. One nerve for the thumb and the pointer and middle finger. The other nerve controls and collects sensation from the ring finger and pinkie finger. I knew that if I didn't have MND then I should have less sensation on the thumb side of my hand.

'I think I felt a difference,' I say. 'Do it again.'

I focused. I tried hard to concentrate to feel a difference; even a tiny difference in feeling could be important. Although I told Dom that I could feel a difference, I really didn't convince myself or him. In the end, the exam didn't provide enough information to give a definitive diagnosis, so I was booked in for a nerve conductance study. Needle electromyography (EMG) to be precise.

For the needle EMG stage, Rachel and I were directed into a small windowless room adjacent to the doctor's waiting room. It was almost empty except for a hospital bed, a computer and a single chair in the corner. The doctor introduced himself and asked me to take a seat on the bed. Rachel sat on the chair opposite. By the time I sat down I realised that I couldn't remember his name. *Was it John?* I thought to myself. *It probably doesn't matter,* I concluded. *Keep the brain space for more important things.* He explained how he would place the needle in a series of muscles and would take one reading with the muscle relaxed, then another with the muscle tense.

He slowly slid the needle into the muscle of my thumb. It was uncomfortable but not particularly painful. Then I had to flex the muscle. The sensation of having a foreign body inside the flexed muscle was akin to scraping your fingernails down a blackboard. My entire body shuddered. From my thumb, he moved to my shoulder, my thigh and calf muscle. The needle seemed to be going deeper and deeper each time. If the reading wasn't looking great he wiggled it around under my skin like he was trying to get reception on his mobile phone. He then repeated the sequence on the left side of my body. After he did the last reading on my leg, I breathed a sigh of relief. 'One last muscle,' he assured me. I had no idea where he was going to stab me next. 'Poke out your tongue,' he said. 'My tongue?' I replied, hoping that he was kidding. 'Yes,' was his simple answer.

I stuck my tongue out as far as it would go and he grabbed it by the tip and inserted the needle in the side of it. A single tear escaped my eye and rolled down my cheek. I felt lost. My tongue hurt but I didn't think that the tear was from the needle. It had been my birthday just a couple of days before. I had just turned forty-two. I should have been celebrating another successful lap around the sun, and instead here I was wondering if I would make it back around again.

Now that the tests were complete, we had enough information for Dom to make a decision on whether this was MND. We found ourselves back in his office sitting exactly where Sarah and Jayson had sat almost a decade ago. My stomach was a bag of nerves and I perceived a slight tremor of my whole body. There would be no pleasant chit-chat on this occasion. I thought that I could hear Rachel's heart beating ever faster over the sounds of the busy clinic outside the office. We were at the crest of the rollercoaster, anticipating the rapid descent to come.

Dom launched straight in as he began to draw a diagram to illustrate his point. 'We can detect active denervation because muscle fibres will have acetylcholine receptors over the whole of the muscle fibre membrane rather than being limited to the neuromuscular junction. This is detected by the EMG needle as a—'

'Dom,' Rachel interrupted. Her voice had a waver to it that revealed a mixture of anger and fear that I had not heard from her before. 'Dom, just tell us. Is it MND?'

'Yes.'

In one word our world imploded.

Rachel let out an agonising cry. The sound of a heart breaking into a thousand pieces.

I sat in silence. Taking in the scene as if it were a movie. Dom sat helpless at his desk. A strange wave of calm washed over me. For the first time in two decades, I didn't have to worry if I would get MND. I didn't have to worry about when I would find out or how I would feel. Two decades of stress and anxiety of the unknown was gone. We finally knew the when and how and I didn't know it yet but my nightmares of being chased were about to stop. It was a brief reprieve; the new uncertainties had not yet had a chance to form and solidify in my mind.

Rachel doubled over sobbing uncontrollably. I held her. Silently.

Now that the news had had a few minutes to sink in, the weight of all those whom I had lost was bearing down on me.

Dom came over to hold Rachel.

When the first shockwaves of our imploding lives had subsided, Dom explained the test results. They had found active denervation in my thumb and only my thumb. Nowhere else. He said it was early but that this meant that it was going to be a slow-progressing form. One of my aunts had had MND for over a decade, so this did not seem impossible. We held on to those words.

I knew one thing. No matter what I felt inside, I had to project strength and calm. I had to be the rock in a raging river. I had to be there for Rachel now because I knew that I couldn't do that for much longer.

We drove home in silence. Holding hands. We had left our old lives behind and when we arrived home it was a new life waiting for us. A life that we didn't choose. A life that we didn't want. But a life nonetheless.

Rachel and I decided we would not tell anyone the news immediately. We had to get used to the idea first. Not that we would ever accept the fact that our lives had shattered but at least we could get past the initial shock before facing the world. It took us till the next day before we could muster the courage to tell the kids. That was the hardest step. What could be harder than telling your children that you are dying of a cruel inherited disease with the implication being that they also have a chance of inheriting the mutation that caused it? No child should have to endure such torture. The mental scars from growing up in this family would be with them forever.

I was reluctant to tell them for many reasons, one of which was that Maddy was in the middle of the HSC. The final year of high school. It is always a stress-filled year and I didn't want to add to that. But it was inevitable.

We asked the girls to come into the living room. We had something to tell them. I wished I knew what they were thinking as they came in and sat down. I recalled what was going through my mind when as a child my parents had called me in to the lounge room to tell me my mum was pregnant. I lived a simpler, more naïve life. It was entirely possible that our daughters already suspected that this talk was going to be about MND in some way.

'I have MND,' I blurted out. They remained silent and tears rolled down their faces as I kept talking. 'My thumb isn't working but that's all. Dom thinks it will be slow. There's a new drug trial starting soon.' I peppered them with reasons why this news wasn't as bad as they may think. I tried to show confidence, strength and calmness because I believed that it would be less traumatic for them. In reality, no one escapes from MND but I had to at least pretend that we could beat this. I realised that in the very best case I may be able to give myself a few extra years, whatever that meant, but I kept this part to myself.

I vowed to live my life as normal as possible. What normal was I could no longer say with any certainty. I guess now what I meant was that I wanted to keep life as similar as possible to what it had been just a few weeks before I had been diagnosed. I didn't stop going to work. Rachel continued to work and the kids kept their routines. It was not that I wanted us to ignore what was happening to me but I needed to keep my research moving, and our normal life gave us some comfort as our old life disintegrated atom by atom.

We began to tell people our news, moving from our inner circle of family then friends. I found myself comforting friends and family as I got around to telling people in person. It was a strange role reversal but I could never have played the victim. I didn't have time to waste. I didn't have time for pity. I knew that some people didn't know what to say to me now that I was dying. I was on the other side of the coin. Just as I didn't know what to say to Ashley all those years ago. But I didn't have time to dwell on that either.

I had to refocus my work on potential therapy. I had already started to pivot the direction of the laboratory work but now the change was more urgent. Not because I thought that what we were doing would be ready to make a difference for me but I had promised my mother, I had promised my sister, and I had promised myself that I would find something to at least slow this disease.

Some people perhaps mistook my stoicism for courage but I was, and am, far from courageous. I remain stubbornly determined and pigheaded with an unjustified confidence that what I am doing can actually make a difference. Many doubt that I can make a real impact, even those closest to me, but I carry on defiantly.

Chapter Sixteen

Looking for Hope

Sitting on the gurney, my legs did not quite touch the floor, so I swung them one at a time back and forth. It had been months since I was diagnosed with MND, and, all things considered, physically I felt okay. Mentally, that was a different story. I tried to put the fact that I was dying to the back of my mind, but in reality it was not that simple. I think that though I did a good job to project calm and confidence, internally I was being tossed back and forth like a rowboat upon the sea in a tempest. I could outwardly rationalise my calmness because the paralysis had stayed contained in my right arm.

I had a freshly inserted cannula on the inside of my elbow in preparation for blood to be taken at intervals over the next twenty-four hours. The room was a sparse clinical space with bare white walls except for a photograph of a man with MND. The man looked happy; perhaps he was even laughing. He had a rubber glove on his head so it looked like a rooster's comb. He had a tracheostomy tube inserted into his throat. He must have been towards the end of his disease. I wondered about this man and what it was that made him so happy while, on the face of it, he was in such a bad situation. I could not conjure a worse situation from my imagination. It made me wonder how I would feel as I stared death in the face. The desk opposite the hospital bed on which I sat was almost bare as well. It seemed like an office that was seldom used. Only a few papers scattered randomly on the desktop and a small orange vial with a single capsule provided any evidence that the space was being used.

'Are you worried?' Dom said, standing by the bed.

I was a bit perplexed. 'Worried?' I replied.

'Yes, worried. You are going to be the first person in the world to ever take this drug at a therapeutic dose.'

I thought about that for a second. 'Well, I wasn't worried until you said that!'

I was about to take the first dose of a drug called copper-ATSM as part of a clinical trial. I had first heard about copper-ATSM at a conference about a decade prior to this trial. It stuck with me because I had never seen a small molecule drug have such a dramatic positive effect on the mice that were genetically modified to get MND. The research team led by Dr Peter Crouch would, over the next decade, test the drug again and again only to reinforce its effectiveness and solidify the drug as a leading candidate to take to clinical trials. From all reports, the drug seemed extremely safe. The researchers maintained that even at extremely high doses there was no toxicity to the mice.

So, I was feeling extremely safe. After all, the mice had taken above one hundred milligrams per kilogram of the drug. Not that we can directly compare effective drug doses between mice and humans in any meaningful way, but per kilogram, the mouse dose was three thousand times higher than the dose I was about to take. The dose contained within the solitary pill sitting across from me was so much lower than what had been given to the mice that it hadn't even registered when Dom asked if I was worried.

If this drug was as potent in humans as it was in mice, then we might expect it to extend life by twenty per cent. Meaning that if I was going to live to the age of fifty without the drug, then it would not be unreasonable to think it might extend my life by ten years. That would not make it a cure, but it would feel like an extra lifetime, given that the drug approved at the time was reportedly extending lives by only two or three months. If it did actually work, it would be a luxury.

I felt privileged to be sitting on that gurney. Not only was I being given an opportunity that my grandmother, mother, sister and other affected relatives were not, but I also appreciated the time that it took to go from the first pilot experiments of a new drug to a pill that you could pop in your mouth. That one small pill sitting at the bottom of that vial represented over a decade of painstaking science. There would have been hours upon hours of dedicated work by dozens of scientists and millions of dollars in research funding that would have gone into getting that one pill ready, so it could be sitting right there in front of me. It was, by this measure, the most expensive pill that I would ever put in my mouth.

It felt like the beginning of a new era. An era where we had started to make real inroads into MND, and into the discovery of drugs to treat it. I thought that if this drug works, then we might just see the floodgates open, and there may be a flurry of new effective therapeutics coming into the clinic. I had put a lot of my hope into this drug. I knew that I only had one shot at an experimental treatment, and I put all my chips on the table for this particular drug. All I could do now was take the drug and hope.

Any thoughts of this drug working to prolong my life or trigger the ushering in of a new era of drug discovery came from the voice of the optimist in my head. The realist inside me knew that while hundreds of molecules were thought to extend the life of the MND mice, not a single one of those drugs went on to be successful in clinical trials for people with MND. Given such poor translation from the laboratory to patients, why did I think that this would be any different? The answer is simple. I had no other choice. In the meantime, we would keep working in the lab on other strategies just in case.

I felt that it was time for my lab to pivot from solely focusing on understanding the underlying biology of MND to at least some of the projects in the lab looking into possible therapies. I had to find out if I could bend science and biology to my will. I had to find out if I had been able to shine enough light so that we could see into the shadows of MND. Had we been able to reveal enough so that we now had adequate knowledge to design therapies?

Our first foray into therapeutic research was through collaborative projects. It was a new era for our laboratory. My thoughts about designing therapies for MND were centred on targeting the actual causative element. While the actual causative agent or factor responsible for the large majority of MND cases is still unknown, the genetic causes in some cases provide a much less murky picture. In the simplest possible terms, a genetic mutation can have two possible effects on a gene. A disease-causing mutation can either result in the loss of the function of the gene, or it can cause the gain of a new and unrelated function. In some complicated circumstances, a genetic mutation can cause both.

In the case of mutations in the SOD1 gene, it had been known for a long time that the mutations caused a toxic gain of function. We and many others had studied what that gain of function was so that we might be able to intervene to quash the effects. However, the closer we looked, the more we understood that these mutations were a molecular cluster bomb that damaged not one but dozens of parts of the cell. This meant that targeting the damage caused by mutant SOD1 would be unlikely to be effective. So it was becoming increasingly clear that we had to target the SOD1 gene or its encoded protein directly to have the best chance of slowing down the disease.

Given that we knew that the SOD1 was accumulating in a form that was not folded properly, we could see two strategies for addressing the issue. The first and perhaps most logical way of addressing the accumulation of SOD1 was to manipulate the biochemistry of SOD1 to reduce the amount in motor neurons. The problem would then become mathematical. If SOD1 was accumulating, it made sense that there was too much of the protein and that reducing the amount of it would reduce the amount that accumulated. The leading way to do this was through the RNA interference that we had been following since Stacey had the conversation with Professor Bob Brown about a decade prior.

It seemed like we were no closer to having the SOD1 antisense therapy available than we were ten years ago. The antisense therapy was being driven forward by the companies Ionis and Biogen. The drug was still in the early phases of its testing. The clinical trial that was ongoing at the time aimed primarily to test the safety of the therapy. The study took place at eighteen sites in the US, Canada and Western Europe, and early results of the trial suggested that the

ASO treatment was safe and reduced mutant SOD1 protein. Most adverse events were mild to moderate. The exploratory trial was designed to measure whether high doses of the drug would prevent neuronal death and impaired functioning, when compared to the placebo group. Initially it seemed to be effective.

The trial seemed to be going well but by no means did it seem like a cure. Theoretically, this treatment should have worked. It was designed to target the fundamental cause of the form of MND associated with mutant SOD1. So it was more than a little disappointing that it was not more obviously effective. Given that this therapy was not an immediate success, one thing that I wondered about was how much of the therapy was getting to where it was needed in motor neurons. After all, the treatment, which consisted of short pieces of DNA, was administered by intrathecal injection into the lumbar spinal cord. So not only was the DNA given naked and left to diffuse into motor neurons, it also had to be invasively injected or infused directly into the spinal cord. It seemed that the therapy was well thought out but that the method of administration could be problematic. The infusion of DNA molecules was likely to be inefficient. The injection into the spine was a particularly invasive procedure that limited the dosage and number of doses able to be delivered.

But how could the delivery of these molecules be improved? I knew that drug delivery was a focus in the field of cancer, unlike in the field of MND, where it seemed an afterthought. MND research was probably twenty or thirty years behind the field of cancer research, if I am being generous. And while on the surface of it, MND is precisely the opposite of cancer, with the former condition characterised by the loss of cells and the latter characterised by the uncontrolled growth of cells, there is much we can learn from cancer research. In fact, I shared an office with a research fellow whose team focused on drug delivery in various cancers. I had known Kara for over a decade at this point, and for the past five years, we had shared an office. Kara's lab worked on a wide range of different ways to get drugs to the part of the body that requires them, from drug-loaded polymers that could be implanted into organs to nanoparticles that target blood cells.

Kara and I had been mulling over the possibility of working together to more efficiently target gene-silencing technology to the nervous system in a way that was minimally invasive. We finally decided to put these ideas in a funding application for a project to start in 2016. The writing of the grant was so last-minute that I showed up at Kara's house late the night before the deadline with my computer and a bottle of red wine. We finished both the wine and the application in the early hours of the next morning and submitted it to the US Department of Defense. It was in January 2016 that we found out that we were successful. Our project would be conducted at our modest University of Wollongong, while the other successful applications that round went to labs in well-known universities such as Stanford and Columbia. We were punching above our weight and excited to get started.

After I had been on the clinical trial for over a month, it was clear that my rate of disease progression was not being affected. This was not surprising, given that the dose of copper-ATSM that I was taking could not even be detected in my blood. The trial was set up so that once a particular dose had been tested for six weeks in six patients and was deemed safe, all participants could then move up a dose. Given that I was the first person to take three milligrams, I would have to wait for twelve people to go through the six-week trials. It was projected that it would be six months before I was able to move up to six milligrams, which was again unlikely to be a big enough dose to make it into the blood in sufficient quantities to be detected there, let alone make it to the brain. Six months to most people is not that long or consequential, but to someone with MND it is. In six months, I had lost the entire use of my right arm. In just six months, we had watched Ashley, Stacey and Sarah go from first symptoms to death. If I wanted any shot at this drug working for me, I would have to bend the rules.

I had always kept a bank account that held tens of thousands of dollars as an emergency fund in case there was a trial or approved drug somewhere in the world that I needed to travel for. I thought that using some of this emergency fund to supplement the trial to get a higher dose would be a good investment. Given that this drug was not something that you could pick up at your local pharmacy, I would have to find someone who would make it. If I told the people running the clinical trial, I would be removed from the trial and, more importantly, the safety monitoring. Despite the risks, I went about giving myself fifty milligrams daily. I would like to add here that I do not recommend that anyone go out and order drugs off the internet. Even drugs that are ninety-nine per cent pure may have impurities that are dangerously toxic. To get around this, I decided to take a fraction of the drug and have it tested in a lab. Obviously, I couldn't tell the lab what I had bought the drug for, so I told them I wanted to check if the drug was protective in the context of whether the SOD1 mutant could still bind copper.

We hypothesised that the copper from copper-ATSM is transferred to the SOD1 protein. The copper helps the protein fold into the right shape. This is important because, in people with MND, SOD1 accumulates in a misfolded and copper-free form. But some mutations that cause MND just so happen to be in the part of the protein that binds to a copper molecule. This means that it can never bind to copper no matter what you do. We realised that if the copper-ATSM was really working in this way, we would find that it did not protect cells containing the mutations that can't bind copper.

It just so happened that we had a student who had signed up to do an internship in the laboratory and was looking for a project. That student just so happened to be my daughter Maddy. Maddy, along with the member of the group who had been with us the longest, Natalie, proved that the drug could not protect cells containing the SOD1 with mutations that no longer supported the binding of copper into the protein. That gave us information on how the drug worked and clues on how to improve it. Another senior member of the group and I wrote a brief paper that suggested that using various drug combinations that targeted different aspects of the folding of SOD1 might increase the effectiveness of the copper-ATSM drug.

We had recently collaborated with labs in Liverpool and Vancouver on different drugs that had the potential to work synergistically with copper-ATSM. Now we just needed to test it.

Chapter Seventeen

The Year of Lasts

At the beginning of 2017, I had reason to be positive. My MND was largely contained within my right arm, the drug from the internet was protecting cells in culture with no obvious toxicity, and taking it did not throw up any red flags with the clinical trial safety monitoring. We were still not talking about the MND and dying in our home, lest death prick up his ears and point his scythe in my direction. Perhaps it was wishful thinking, but we truly had no inkling of the traumatic twelve months that were in store for us.

The year began as years always began for us, or at least it seemed that it had always been that way. Rachel and I had been making an almost annual pilgrimage to Jervis Bay's Booderee National Park. The leafy campsite, white sands and tranquil turquoise waters held us in their thrall, which kept us coming back year after year, regardless of whatever part of the world we had been exploring. We first started visiting the bay before our daughters were born, and over the years we had shared this little paradise with different groups of friends. This year was not that different from previous visits except our friend Glen wasn't able to come as he was undergoing chemotherapy. My paralysed arm was no more than a nuisance as we marched down to the beach, clambered over rocks and went on bushwalks.

Then, one fine morning, on our twenty-fifth anniversary, after Rachel reminded me that she would love me no matter what was to come, the protective armour that I had built up around myself, thickened by my resolve that I could continue to work and live normally despite the deep scars seared into my brain, shattered. An overwhelming number of thoughts came flooding in. So many I couldn't discern any one particular thought. I found that the reality of my inescapable fate left me sobbing. Uncontrollable, body-shaking sobs. I was in free fall, and the gravity of it all took my breath away. I clung to Rachel so that I would not lose myself.

What we could not have foreseen, or perhaps what we didn't want to see, was that it would be our last camping trip to Booderee. In fact, I have come to think of 2017 as my year of lasts. Beginning with our last trip to Booderee, my decline could be charted by the series of moments in which it became clear that it would be the last time that I would be able to do a particular thing.

In late January, we embarked upon our last big family adventure. As a family, we loved adventurous trips around the world. I cherished every experience more than I did the destinations. While I loved exploring the amazing architecture and tasting the local cuisine of every corner of the globe, my most memorable moments were the things like playing barefoot football with kids from a remote village in the mountains of Thailand or sipping the homemade liquor of a man who lived on the water's edge in Croatia as he explained to me how he survived the bloody war in 1991. These moments of connection that crossed the boundaries of language and culture were very human moments and were something that I would have once shied away from as a shy young man but now cherished. So, it was not a question of whether we would travel but where we would travel while I still could.

It didn't take too long for us to choose a destination. Rachel and I knew that a trip somewhere on the African continent was going to be the top of the list because it was a part of the world that we had not explored. We made plans to visit the Okavango Delta and the Kalahari Desert in Botswana and Kruger National Park in South Africa. The trip would not have been possible even a few weeks later, as I was already having trouble climbing into the back of the safari truck. It was becoming clear that my left arm was beginning to weaken. It didn't impinge on our trip, but in the back of my mind I knew MND was rumbling along, and in a way it felt like all my efforts were futile, like a lone man trying to hold back a wave coming into the shore.

While the natural aspects of the trip were spectacular and the wildlife was a sight to behold, it was the lessons that I learnt along the way that have stuck with me. For example, the trip crystallised the idea that life can be brutal. We saw a pack of wild painted dogs cross in front of us, carrying parts of what looked like a young antelope. It was a moment that reminded me that my plight was no different from any other life on the planet. Life is fragile and the forces of nature can be brutal and beautiful at the same time.

For the first time I also got a deeper understanding of the inequality that persists in South Africa. We had paid a local guide from Soweto to give us a bit of a history tour around Johannesburg. I had obviously heard about apartheid but seeing infamous locations first-hand was an emotionally charged experience. One memorial in particular brought it home for me. I knew that the government had put quotas in place to ensure that, going forward, resources would be distributed more equally. But what had not occurred to me was that under apartheid, black South Africans could not own property. This meant that all of the property wealth was still in the hands of the white minority and it would take countless generations to balance out. If I was looking for evidence that the world was an unfair place, I needn't look any further. I certainly felt that I was privileged and, despite my condition, could not expect or ask for any sympathy.

In February, I managed the last song on my guitar. I was no musician but could strum a few chords that I had taught myself. Playing the guitar was a hobby that was a type of meditation and I often played just for myself and occasionally for others, and we would sing along during these times. The resonance of a chord on a finely tuned guitar felt right in a way that I couldn't put into words. The vibrations of the strings was reminiscent of our lives – each of the family doing their own thing but together we were in harmony. As my right arm became increasingly paralysed, the strumming had become difficult and clumsy. Not only did this affect the music but increasingly it affected the harmony in our family. Because of the very obvious changes to my ability to make a song sound right, I had stopped playing altogether. So it was a surprise that on this particular evening in February 2017 I picked up the guitar and doubly surprising that I found it possible to strum. I could immediately tell that this would be a very temporary reprieve so I had to carefully choose the last song I would ever play. I chose a duet with Maddy. It was our favourite song to sing together – 'Little Talks' by the Icelandic band Of Monsters and Men. We had sung the song dozens of times but I had never felt the words cut as deeply as that evening while Maddy sang one of the particularly poignant verses about someone who's gone away, leaving only a ghost.

During March, I had my last ride on my mountain bike. I had been riding on various trails on the Illawarra escarpment with friends or with Rachel for the past decade. The difficulty of the trail governed who I rode with. Rachel and I had been riding a less challenging trail every weekend, and it was on that trail that I was still able to ride with Rachel after my diagnosis. We kept mountain biking despite the doctors' warnings that this was extremely dangerous. I would strap my bad hand to the handlebar and away we would go. I knew that a fall from my bike could be fatal if I could not protect my head by cushioning the fall with my arms. By that point my right arm was basically lifeless and now my left arm was noticeably weaker, so I knew I would soon have to make a decision to stop.

Losing motor neurons and the subsequent disconnection of the muscles from the brain is surprisingly painless. At least there is no physical pain. The loss of arm function means the increasing loss of independence, which, while not associated with physical hurt, is associated with angst and inner turmoil. Another indirect result of the muscles in my arms wasting away was the complication that my shoulders could no longer support my arm, leaving it in a permanent state of dislocation. But the pain and distress were not confined to me. I can only imagine the various heartbreaks Rachel experienced watching my decline.

So, one Saturday I decided that this was going to be my last bike ride. We gathered a small group of friends together and we set off from our place for the last time. We rode the same route that had been a weekend staple for Rachel and me. We would set off west until the houses of the suburbs gave way to farms before cutting through a hole in the fence to ride along the track at the side. Previously we had come across snakes, echidna and even deer but on this last trek I had to settle for the company of friends, with the spectacular views of the mountains to the west and the lake and ocean to the east. I had previously taken the beauty of the environment for granted but that day I soaked it in, knowing that I would not see this trail ever again.

In April, we planned our last trip to Cambridge. Cambridge felt like our second home, and we didn't know when or if we would ever get back there. I had been travelling to Cambridge once or twice a year over the past decade and we had lived there as a family on three occasions. We had dear friends there and my friend and mentor Chris Dobson was Master of St John's College, so he rolled out the red carpet for our visit. We had almost unlimited access to the college and visited the Master's Lodge and the old library with its ornate wooden shelves bulging with leather-bound books.

St John's had arranged a house for us to stay in close to the college on St John's Road. The only issue was the stairs. While I could manage the climb to the third-floor bedroom, we were concerned with how steep the stairs were and the consequences for me if I fell. So, I needed an escort front and back each time I ascended and descended the staircase. We also managed a walk along the Cam to the orchard in Grantchester. It was a beautiful walk but for the first time I really noticed my legs fatigue. As we had much more walking around the city to do, I was concerned.

Probably the thing that I was most looking forward to in Cambridge was a meeting with Stephen Hawking. Without my knowledge, my office mate, Kara, had written to Chris Dobson's personal assistant, Karen, to see if it was possible for me to meet with Stephen. Karen had passed on the message to Chris as he had recently met Stephen and his ex-wife Jane during the filming of the screen adaptation of Jane's memoir. So, it was arranged that we would meet Stephen at his house on Good Friday.

We walked from St John's, along the Backs, through the crisp morning air with each breath visible and a soft mist rising from the channels of the Cam through the colleges. There was an anxious energy in our party as we entered Stephen's front garden. As we stood on the doorstep waiting for someone to answer the bell, I wondered what he would be like.

We had been cautioned that the reality of meeting Stephen Hawking was far from his polished appearances on TV and that his current condition could be confronting. I don't know what I was expecting but the ordinariness of the scene that greeted us was disarming and it settled our nerves. The room was a warm yellowy colour, well-lit from the large timber windows framed by green curtains. Several pictures hung on the wall including family photographs. Despite the warnings and the awkward initial introductions, Stephen was engaging and genuinely interested in the conversations we were having, seated around his dining table.

I explained to him that it was hard to tell people how badly life-limiting motor neurone disease is, when Stephen had lived with it for more than fifty years. He appreciated the irony. Stephen was interested to hear about the work that we were doing. I told him that the microscopic hallmark of MND/ALS is the protein deposits within motor neurons, and to think of the deposits as tiny black holes that can swallow up hundreds of proteins, and that the information about the proteins is then lost. I like to think that after our conversation Stephen imagined having tiny black holes in his brain.

After two hours of deep conversation with Stephen, it was time to go. One of his nurses told me Stephen wanted to shake my hand. I turned to see her holding his right hand up. I held out my left hand, and said, 'Sorry, my right is not my good hand.' She looked at me and said, 'It's not Stephen's good hand either.' So, we shook hands with assistance.

After being forewarned about the confronting nature of Stephen's condition, I walked away from the house, not repulsed but inspired by the fact that even fully paralysed Stephen was able to contribute. It raised my spirits.

After leaving Cambridge I had a chance to reflect on the trip, and the reality that I would never again walk the streets of Cambridge set in. The heady exhilaration of scientific discussions, the gritty texture of the centuries-old buildings, the haunting sounds of the evensong bouncing off the vaulted ceilings and the smells of the college gardens were left behind forever – just as I had to leave behind the full functionality of my arms and everything that I once took for granted that I did with them. I cannot adequately put into words the depth of my sadness at what I had already left behind.

I was acutely aware during my year of lasts that my ability to do a particular task would disappear as soon as I stopped doing it. The mantra of the brain plasticity literature, 'use it or lose it', rang painfully true. I think that this knowledge meant that I really pushed myself too far. I could not see it while I was in the moment but my dogged determination to push things to the limit meant that we were not prepared for change when it came and we were reactive instead of proactive.

By May, we had decided that it was no longer possible for Rachel to do everything for me. But because of my desire to keep whatever independence I had for as long as possible, I was just not prepared for changes. I felt that while I was in the office, I didn't need any assistance. This was true initially. I had help to get to work and then again to get home, but once I was at my desk, I felt that having a support worker looking over my shoulder was an unnecessary cramping of my style. After all, I did have someone already looking out for me. My office mate and long-term friend Kara was, I thought, prepared to do little bits and pieces that I would need. I should never have presumed that this was the case. It was not fair to put this responsibility on her. I could not see it at the time but I was in the process of just getting through the day and I expected too much and never stopped to ask if it was okay with her.

One day Kara had left the office for a meeting and she returned to find me stuck in an awkward position. I had dropped one of my raspberry-flavoured treats on the floor and without too much thought I had crouched down to pick it up. I knew that I would not be able to pull myself up with my feeble arms but I didn't realise that my legs were not going to be able to get me back up. When Kara stepped back into the office, she found me squatting and leaning on the side of my desk. It didn't take long to figure out that I was stuck, but getting me upright when my centre of gravity was so low was not as straightforward as it seemed. As she tried to lift me, we toppled to the floor. It was impossible now for Kara to help me up from my position of lying face-up on the floor. I felt like a helpless overturned turtle. Kara fetched some reinforcements and I was back up on my chair in no time. I was a little embarrassed and nursing a bruised ego but had otherwise avoided injury. It was, though, the last time I tried to pick something up off the floor.

Soon after I had been scraped up off the floor, I found myself in an urgent and even more embarrassing situation. Even though my arms were almost no longer any use, with some ingenuity and elasticised pants I could manage to take myself to pee. That is until the day I went into the bathroom and could no longer move my trousers, no matter what I did. I thought I had two options in the moment. I could stand there and pee in my pants or I could ask someone to help. I went back to the office and tentatively asked Kara for help. She said yes, so long as she did not have to hold it. It was the last time I took myself to the toilet.

Losing control of my hands would have larger repercussions than just being able to move my pants. I would also lose my ability to type on my computer. The MND was rapidly taking away my independence. I had been a very private person but if I wanted to keep working and if I wanted Rachel to keep some sense of her own life and career, I would have to get over my own sense of privacy and embarrassment. At work I had never been busier. So, I had to figure out a way to keep writing. I switched from typing to voice control.

In July we took our last family holiday. We chose Fiji. I did my last walk of any substantial distance. We walked to a nearby village. I didn't make it all the way back. I had to get a chair brought to me fifty metres from the resort. I could not make it any further. With the help of a young Fijian man, I managed my last snorkel. One day in the bure, I had a bad fall and hit my head on the wall on the way down. We needed help to get me up.

In August, I fell trying to get out of the car at work. We needed three people to pick me up from the ground. The next time I came into work a wheelchair was waiting for me. It was the last time I walked into work. My colleague and friend Neil Cashman suggested that I have a think about whether I would like to be ventilated through a tracheostomy tube.

In September, Rachel and I, with a small group of friends, went on a last-ditch weekend away. We visited the Penfolds winery in South Australia and did some wine blending. I didn't manage to get any sleep that weekend as I started to struggle for breath. It was a frightening development.

Back home, as I was making the small number of steps from the shower to the bed, I felt particularly unstable and, even though Rachel was holding me, realised I was not going to be able to stay upright. Rachel had to call out for help to Talia and her partner, Tyler. We were devastated, but I now had to start using a hoist to lift me and a BiPAP ventilator to help me breathe. I found the BiPAP mask uncomfortable and painful to wear.

We had been very social and had often entertained dozens of people at our home. For the last time we held a large soirée. It felt like a farewell. I had too much wine for the last time. I did not have the muscles to vomit but was terrified that if I did it would fill my lungs.

In among my year of lasts, I had a first. I had my first panic attack.

I awoke in a wave of panic. I called out, but no sound escaped my mouth, and my limbs didn't respond to my pleas for them to move. Uncharacteristically, I spiralled very quickly around and around between trying to scream out and waves of panic until it all came to an abrupt end when an unaware and perfectly calm Rachel walked back into the room. Her mere presence was calming, like it had been so many times before and would be so many times afterwards. In addition to the anxiety attack, I had a moment of crystal-clear insight that night. This is not where I thought my life would be at this time. It wasn't supposed to be like this.

The year 2017 was a rollercoaster ride. In the dark. Travelling at breakneck speed. Backwards. Starting with the camping trip, the year would be unsettling and disorienting. We never knew what was coming and, as a result, we had no time to get used to a particular direction before the next corner threw us about.

The year had one last twist. I was told I had only a few months to live. There was only one option if I wanted to stay alive. Surgery. And a tracheostomy tube in my throat with mechanical ventilation. It would also mean I would be disqualified from continuing on the copper-ATSM trial. We made the decision to go ahead with the surgery without really understanding what it would mean for our lives.

Chapter Eighteen

My Own Personal Black Hole

As my eyes gradually opened and the darkness gave way to the light, the world filled with a haziness that hung in the air like a thick soup. It was a struggle to move the parts of me that still worked, and evidently the soup had infiltrated my brain because my thoughts were laboured and muddled. Where am I? I asked myself. As the fog began to lift, I took in my surroundings. I was in a hospital bed facing a double glass door. One of the walls to the side was half glass, while the opposite wall was a dark shade of pink. There was little else in the room but a hand-washing station and a rack overflowing with boxes of rubber gloves. Before I could finish the stocktake of what was around me, the surgeon casually strolled into the room. His brown leather shoes seemed too long and out of proportion. I realised that this was probably not the important detail of his visit, but my brain wouldn't let it go.

Before he reached the bedside, it hit me. I had survived the surgery, and I no longer had the mask on my face to help me breathe. The rise and fall of my chest were now totally reliant on the tube that entered my body through the new hole in my throat and the steady whir of the mechanical ventilator to which I was now forever tethered as if it were a plastic umbilical cord. This realisation made me smile, which prompted the surgeon to remark that I must be happy to see him. I had just had surgery to remove my voice box, which allowed for the total and complete separation of my trachea and oesophagus. The reason for this version of the drastic surgery was that MND eventually affects the muscles that help keep food and drink down one passage and air from breathing down another. Eventually, one can literally drown in one's own saliva.

The impact of having my larynx removed was immediately evident. I could no longer speak. In those first buoyant moments after waking from the surgery, I did not fully appreciate the implications of this loss. Rachel and the girls had been dreading the loss of my voice, but I had been more ambivalent. After all, without strength in my muscles associated with breathing, I did not have the ability to speak with any gusto. But the trauma that I had not foreseen started almost immediately. It became clear very quickly that I could not get the attention of the nurses. I was unable to activate the nurse call button because my hands were paralysed, and nor could I call for help without a voice.

I had never felt so vulnerable. Very soon after surgery, this vulnerability would trigger an anxiety in me beyond anything I had experienced before. One evening I had a casual nurse who didn't really know enough about my background. He had decided that what I needed was to be put on my side to avoid getting bed sores despite my muted protests. In order for me to use the one communication device that I had, my eye-gaze system, I needed to be looking straight at the computer, so, by turning me to the side against my will, he cut me off from the world of communication. It was after midnight, so the lights were off in the ICU. The only light in the room came from the screens of the various bits of machinery that cast a ghostly veil of blue light over the room. Not enough light to see my face and the stress-fuelled contortions that fell across it.

I didn't want to fall asleep like this because if I woke up later and needed my airway cleared, I wouldn't be able to get his attention. I tried to call out, but the words that left my mouth fell flat on the floor. Even now, it is hard to put into words the feeling of complete vulnerability and utter helplessness that I felt in that moment.

I had my life given over to someone that I didn't know or trust. I felt that I had lost control over my life, and that scared the shit out of me.

As my anxiety levels peaked, I noticed that the nurse was approaching me. I felt a wave of relief start to wash over me. At last, my stress had been recognised, and I would be able to sleep. To my dismay, the nurse didn't acknowledge me but instead proceeded to disconnect my ventilator tubing. I could no longer breathe, and no matter how much I tried, I could not get my message across.

I CANNOT BREATHE!

I entered an unrivalled panic attack. I had no idea how to get his attention and tell him that I could not breathe.

I CANNOT BREATHE!

My struggle to communicate only resulted in the more rapid depletion of my oxygen stores. Eventually, still oblivious to my distress, my tubing was reconnected, and I could breathe again.

I would later find out that he thought that the vital sensor in the tubing that controls the pressure and exhalation of my breathing was a nebuliser, and he had tried to remove it. The only thing that he achieved was the stripping of any trust I had in the nurses and the setting of my baseline levels of stress at an unsustainable level. My heart rate stayed above 115 beats per minute for several weeks. Likely as a consequence of these elevated levels of stress, I now have almost no memory of the first three months of my stay in the hospital. I have a handful of memories that are incomplete, and I don't have a sense of how they fit into the chronological order of the events.

Stephen Hawking wrote that the twelve months following his tracheostomy were his own personal black hole. I now understand what he meant by that. Not even memories made it out of my own black hole. Although I cannot remember, there are things that I know happened during my time living in the ICU. After my initial panic, the only person in the world that I totally trusted was Rachel. I would not have survived without her. I clung to her like a frightened child gripping the leg of a parent. But the fact that I needed her by my side left her in a kind of limbo where she put everything on hold for me and had to rent a room near the hospital. It must have been exhausting, and combined with my continued deterioration, it must have been a thankless and depressing time for her.

The first complication was the fact that I did not take well to being fed through the nasogastric tube that was taped to my nose. My digestive system couldn't tolerate the constant flow of the liquid diet directly into my stomach. I was in constant pain from the cramping. I was also starving without nearly enough calories. I lost forty kilograms over the three months and got as low as sixty-seven kilograms. As a very tall man, I had not been that weight since I was fourteen years old.

A potentially bigger problem was that the site of the surgery would not heal. I had a fistula or abscess that was leaking from the back of my throat on to my chest. They tried putting a funnel down my throat to bypass the pesky hole, and, when that didn't work, they tried higher and higher doses of a drug to dry out my saliva. This only resulted in my bladder, kidneys and bowels shutting down and making me delusional from the pain. In the end, it was all for naught, and I had to have a second surgery.

On top of everything else, Rachel began the first of our fights for funding by the EnableNSW Home Ventilation Scheme, without which there was no prospect of me coming home. She must have been wondering if this was worth all the time and effort. My quality of life had, up to this point, been poor, and I was physically and mentally incapable of thinking about anything but getting through the next hour. But Rachel never gave up on me and she always fiercely defended and protected me. I will never be able to repay her.

It was six months before I made it home from the ICU. I had sometimes wondered if I would ever make it. I had also wondered if we made the right decision to prolong my life with the surgery. Life had been harder than I ever could have imagined, and I would not return home the same person as before with just an extra hole in my throat. How could I possibly have been the same person? What kept me going was Rachel's strength and my deep-rooted desire to protect the kids from this terrible disease. Like jumping into the ocean to save Talia from a rip, it was my automatic response. I didn't expect to be the one that finds the cure to MND but if I could add one valuable piece to the puzzle, then I had to keep trying. I could not just give up. I had to keep going, no matter the cost to me personally.

By July 2018, my health had stabilised, and we had a team of support workers trained to look after me. We finally could plan for my homecoming. I was nervous. I had consulted daily with doctors in the ICU for the last six months, which gave me a kind of comfort knowing that I could rely on them to pick up and treat any issues. I had had several bouts of pneumonia by this stage and seemingly had a colony of pseudomonas (bacteria) in my lungs that would not go away. I didn't know how to live at home anymore, but at the same time I knew that being in the ICU was not a life. While it would never really be the same as the life we'd known before when living together as a family, given I would need round-the-clock care, necessitating people coming and going at all hours, this was a new chance for me to see the girls grow into women. And a new chance to continue my research, which had been in a holding pattern for six months.

Sadly, the copper-ATSM that I had been taking for over a year seemed to have had no effect on the progress of my MND, despite the promise of the drug in every test we and others had tried. After rapidly losing much of my ability to move in 2017, I had only really stabilised because I had very little left to lose. Despite my profound disability, our laboratory published twenty papers across 2017–2018. We had been more productive in those two traumatic years than in any other two-year period since we had begun MND research. It just goes to show how dedicated my team of researchers was – and still is.

Given the fact that the copper-ATSM seemed not to have slowed my disease but, at the same time, had been so effective in laboratory experiments, we began to think of ways to improve its effectiveness. Our first idea was to complement the drug with other molecules that we had been working on. We thought that targeting slightly different aspects of SOD1 folding would provide us with a synergistic combination. The main problem was that for the first time in over ten years, I had no money coming into the laboratory for projects or my salary. Our research grants had been unsuccessful. This should not have come as a surprise, given the personal torture that I had been through over the previous two years. I thought that it was possible that my time in research was coming to an end. I had to be realistic. I was now profoundly disabled with an uncertain life expectancy. I recognised that I could be perceived as a risk that a funding agency might not be willing to take.

I was not about to give up, though. After all I had been through, and all I had put my family through, this problem of having no funding support seemed trivial. I had to find a way to keep our work going until the next round of funding to give us a chance to keep the lab afloat. The first thing that helped us get through this period was the fact that the university appointed me to a professorial post in January 2019. I became the University of Wollongong's Professor in Neurodegenerative Disorders. The next fortuitous event was the settlement agreement that we made with a large cruise-ship company that had refused me entry from the dock in March 2019, because of my disability. As a result, we worked with them to improve their procedures and also a large sum was donated to our research. Next, an anonymous donor left us a six-figure sum and hundreds of smaller donations were made. Lastly, what else occurred that allowed us to keep going in 2019 was the fact that one of the senior members of the lab, Luke McAlary, was awarded a fellowship in August 2019 that covered his salary. So, with the support of the university and the generous support of the community, we managed to keep the core of the group together.

It was during that precarious period of 2019 that we began to test our drug combination in mice. I will point out here that we don't use animals lightly. It is a necessary part of medical research that therapies are tested in animals prior to humans, to provide evidence that the drug is not toxic and still works the way you think it should in a complex living system. With this in mind, we started by treating the MND mice with a relatively high dose of copper-ATSM and small doses of our other two drugs. To our disappointment, the high dose of copper-ATSM proved toxic. This was a surprise, given that no toxicity had previously been reported. We soon began to hear rumours that the trial in humans had been halted because of toxicity in some people, despite the promise of the early results. This was a huge setback. Not only for the drug, but also for the way we test drugs in general. At the same time, we were testing the use of nanoparticles to deliver the anti-SOD1 antisense therapy to cells. We showed that we could improve the delivery of the antisense therapy in cell culture experiments. When we packaged up the antisense molecules into the nanoparticles and injected them into the bloodstream of zebra fish, we saw that some made it to the motor neurons. The results were promising but we were still a long way away from developing the technology to a point where we could use it in humans.

In 2019, while we had begun to look for a way to more efficiently deliver the therapy, Biogen began a Phase 3 efficacy trial of the antisense therapy. Although I thought that the therapy could be improved upon, I had put a lot of faith in the strategy because it was obvious to me that the disease resulted from the accumulation of the protein. So, if we could reduce the amount of the protein, it should slow or even stop the disease. When the initial results of the trial showed that the SOD1 protein in cerebrospinal fluid was halved by treatment, I was encouraged that this could be the first treatment to really slow the disease. To my dismay, Biogen announced that the trial missed its primary endpoint of slowing disease-associated decline. They reported that treatment was associated with a slight improvement compared to placebo, but it fell short of statistical significance.

To add insult to injury, I had been notified that my application to the NHMRC had been unsuccessful. I felt that everything that I had done was for naught and that perhaps I didn't understand the disease as much as I thought I did. It had taken two decades of my life to get to this point. Almost half of my life had been spent trying to understand this monster of a disease and I feared that all I thought I knew, all that I had built and all that I had gained, was disintegrating before my eyes. I had missed out on funding, and of the two treatments that I thought should be the most promising, one turned out to be toxic at higher doses and the other didn't charge the course of the disease, even though it seemed to do what it was designed to do. It was as if everything that I thought I knew with certainty was not set in stone but was instead a sandcastle melting under the incoming tide.

Chapter Nineteen

Into the Twilight

As I lay there, I was aware of voices. But they sounded distant. They had a tinny quality to them. I couldn't respond; we were past that moment. It had been three minutes since I was accidentally disconnected from my ventilator. Time had slowed, so the three minutes felt like ten. Either way, it was too many minutes without air in my lungs. I was aware of my heart monitor screaming, 'Heart rate critically high,' but it also now seemed somewhere off in the distance.

I could feel my heartbeat. Boom. Boom. Boom. It didn't tally with the 140 beats per minute that my monitor showed. The truth was that I knew that the two people who were looking after me were not going to be able to problem-solve fast enough to save me now. I knew that in the first thirty seconds without air.

So, this is how it ends, I thought to myself. I had imagined that I would gasp and that my body would contort and convulse in a last futile attempt to get some air in my lungs. But there was nothing. Just the slowing of time until it almost completely stopped and the gradual dimming of the light.

Not long now, I thought, while the two support workers fumbled through boxes of equipment that couldn't save me. I let the curtain of darkness start its descent. In the hazy distance, a voice said, 'Should I get Rachel?' I didn't respond, so she asked again. 'Justin, should I get Rachel?' Upon hearing Rachel's name, things began to come into focus. I could hear the alarms and the panicked voices clearly as they screeched back to full speed. My heart sounded like a train at full speed, clacking over the tracks.

B-bom b-bom b-bom.

My eyes, now wide, flickered in the affirmative. I understood with clarity that Rachel would be able to save me.

Within seconds of entering the room, she identified the problem. A few seconds later, the air gushing from the ventilator filled my lungs, and the light came back into the room, pushing the darkness away.

This was not the first time Rachel saved the day, and I'm sure it won't be the last. I have lost count of all the times when Rachel has advocated for me, fought for me, protected me, comforted me and saved my life in both a physical and emotional sense. Rachel is the hero of my story in so many ways. I wish I could be there for her in the same way.

It breaks my heart that I can't. I wish I could be her hero.

I have had a handful of times that I would consider to be genuine near misses. But somehow, this one felt different. I felt that this was closer to death than the others, but I can't put my finger on the exact reason for this. Perhaps it's a probability thing. The more serious issues I have, the more likely the disease is to kill me. I feel that, at some point, my luck will run out. This latest incident, more than anything else in the last six years, has me properly thinking about the end of my life. This has already triggered some tough conversations. I knew from the beginning of this journey that this day would come. After all, I have always known that my MND would continue to progress just as the ventilation would continue to keep my body alive.

Setting up a dilemma that I have to face.

I know that because of the ventilation I will be kept alive past any reasonable point of decline. I will have to make a decision to actively remove therapy. I don't know what scares me more, staying alive too long and not being able to communicate, or deciding to turn off my ventilation.

The despair associated with this moment and the hopelessness of this dilemma was captured four hundred years ago by Shakespeare when he wrote in *Hamlet*, 'To be, or not to be, that is the question'. To live or not. That was Hamlet's famous question. The same question that I am now tussling with. I am not sure that I could have articulated the heart of this dilemma as eloquently as Shakespeare when he wrote:
Whether 'tis nobler in the mind to suffer

The slings and arrows of outrageous fortune,
Or to take arms against a sea of troubles,
And by opposing end them? To die: to sleep.

In those few lines of text, Shakespeare reaches out across the centuries, grabs my heart and pulls it, still beating, from my chest. Somehow, he understood the shared humanity that is timeless. I somehow feel less alone in my dilemma. While Shakespeare identified and recognised the issue, he did not leave us with a path to take or even a way to decide which path to take. I have suffered my fair share of slings and arrows, but how do I know when enough is enough? How am I supposed to decide? Part of Shakespeare's genius was his ability to present an argument without prejudice so that the audience could decide themselves. To Rachel's frustration, I would use this style of learning when raising our daughters. I would prefer to let them come to their own conclusions about what was the right way to do something rather than tell them explicitly what to do. It has become a family joke, but I like to think that I have helped the girls become the amazing independent people they are.

Since the bard can't help with my decision, I have to come up with my own personal strategy. I have an equation that I balance in my head to tell me if I can keep going. I have to be able to say that the things that I live for outweigh the cost of the way I live. I don't have a mathematical way to calculate the answer to my existential dilemma. I hope that if I make a list of the costs of how I live and I compare that to a list of my reasons for living, the answer will be obvious.

I am writing this in November 2022 and can tell you how I feel I am progressing.

First, my cost of living. By the year 2020, my condition had declined so much that I thought I would be stable because I thought that I had reached a point where I had probably lost as much as I could possibly lose. Stephen Hawking managed to live like this for decades. But for me life was already hard. I could not do anything for myself and needed round-the-clock monitoring. I had never had so many people around me, and yet I had never been so lonely. What I didn't realise was that I did have more to lose: my humanity.

I had lost the ability to eat and drink. These were two of my favourite things to do, and both were tied strongly to a sense of what it is to be a human. I didn't realise how much this would affect me. My last solid meal was a lasagne that my dad had made. If you had asked me what I wanted to have as a last meal, I would take my dad's lasagne every time. It was more than a meal. It was a story thirty years in the making. When I was eleven, I had stayed the weekend with the family of a friend. The family were Italian, so I really noticed the difference in the meals compared to my family's. At home, we had the stereotypical meat and three veg. Most often sausages, but only from Pattinson's butchery, or lamb chops with potatoes and carrots. I realise that that is only two vegetables, but they were the two constants. The Italian food that had blown my mind on that trip was called lasagne. I told my mum about this amazing thing. She got the recipe and gave it her own twist. It became a family favourite. My dad carried on the tradition after my mother's death, and it was his lasagne that was my last solid meal. In the end, every time I had a mouthful, the food would end up in my nasal cavity. After a couple of days, it was clear that I would never swallow again, so I was taken to the hospital to have a feeding tube inserted.

Soon after this, the rest of my facial muscles deteriorated. It was not long before I could not even smile. I didn't stop to think about the fact that I couldn't smile until I had a visit from Neil Cashman from Canada. My dear friend said that he wanted to ask me some serious questions. I really respect Neil as a clinician, researcher and friend, so I was happy to have some hard conversations.

He started by explaining how a significant portion of people living with MND who have had a tracheostomy tube inserted to prolong their life would develop depression. 'How are you feeling?' he asked. 'Really, how are you doing?'

I typed my response with my eye gaze. Click. Click. 'OK' was my simple reply.

He probed further. 'Do you feel happiness?'

I was not prepared for this question. I don't think that I have ever been asked that question by anyone in any context. I had to think about it. What is happiness? I conjured up as many happy memories as I could. One thing struck me as being part of every happy memory that I have ever had. I composed my answer letter by letter. 'I don't know if you can be happy if you can't smile,' I replied.

We left it at that.

As my voluntary muscles shut down one by one, I consoled myself with the fact that the muscles that control eye movement are resistant to the effects of MND. It is a phenomenon that is not questioned in the field and much work has aimed to understand the difference between the motor neurons that control eye movement and all others. So, it was a devastating setback when I started noticing that my eyes were weakening. It shook my whole sense of how sustainable this way of living is. My eyes are the window to my world. Every interaction with everyone in my life is through my eyes. If something happens to my eyes, that could very well be the end of me. It was while Rachel was away hiking with her father that it happened. And it wasn't what I expected. One day my eyelids would no longer close properly. I had now progressed further in a handful of years than Stephen Hawking had in half a century. Consider this: in the last four years, the disease has stripped me of every last voluntary muscle, including those used to eat, drink, smile, breathe and eventually those that gave me the ability to close my eyes.

I can't even close my damned eyes.

The result of this loss was a hellish nightmare of an existence. Without the ability to close my eyes, I could not sleep. I can see why keeping people awake has been used as a form of torture. A few days into my inability to sleep, I was confused about where I was and I had started hallucinating. The longest a person has ever lived without sleep is eleven days. Things were looking grim at this point.

We were told that it was possible to get some sleep with one eye closed so we taped down one eye at a time. This was an improvement, but only just. I was still having hallucinations that mingled and intertwined with reality. A family of giant spiders had moved into my bedroom. They were large, half a metre long, with black and orange striped spindly legs. Apart from their fantastical appearance, there were no other clues that they were not real. The spiders climbed on, around and behind the ceiling fan seamlessly and without any evidence that they only existed in my mind. Another recurring hallucination was the gradual filling of the room with water until it lapped gently against the side of the bed. The lack of sleep also sapped my energy, meaning that everything became an order of magnitude harder. The fact that I could not keep my eyes from drying out meant that the cornea was damaged so that I could no longer read without glasses.

This way of living would only be a short-term way to survive and not sustainable for any significant amount of time. Fortunately, we found a longer-term solution. We consulted with an optical surgeon who said that he may be able to help. He performed the surgery with me conscious and Rachel holding my hand. The surgeon inserted weights inside my eyelids that he thought would make it easier to keep my eyes closed. Since the surgery, I still have a lot of trouble closing my eyes and need eye drops around the clock but at least I can keep my eyes closed to get large stretches of sleep.

Apart from all the physical symptoms, I am tired. So tired that the word doesn't quite capture what it is that I feel. Neither does exhausted, fatigued, weary or drained. I have not ever felt like this. I get the feeling that my time is running out. What does that even mean? I have been dying for six years now, but something feels different. My fatigue is almost all-encompassing. For the last few months, I have only had a few lucid hours in the day that I can work or write. By the time the evening comes around when I should be spending time in conversation with my family, instead I am so fatigued that I can barely type out a full sentence.

The closest people around me have learned to get by with a kind of shorthand and one-word dad jokes. I am devastated that I can't give them more but I feel lucky that they have not given up on me.

Now you must be wondering, what is it then that keeps me alive? It is not born from fear. I am not afraid of dying – perhaps I was once, but no longer. In fact, when that day comes, in some ways it will be a relief. To understand why I persist with this life despite the year-long list of challenges we must now look at my list of reasons to live, and make sure that this outweighs the challenges – the costs of the disease – that I live with.

A big part of my motivation or reasons why I keep going that balance the 'to be or not to be' equation is the ability to spend time with family and friends. What is life for if not to spend time with the ones that you love. The problem with having this as a reason to live is that with my ability to communicate being greatly diminished, the quality of the interactions is low. Along with the physical ability to move, I have lost the ability to be a friend and a husband. In fact, I have lost most of what it means to be human.

I am keenly aware of the burden that I have become and the hurt my continuing existence causes. I am happy with just being present while the activity of the family goes on around me. But I realise that this is a selfish notion. Every day is a struggle to feel somewhat okay so that I can continue to do my work, but I sacrifice my dignity and independence and the privacy of my family in the process. No one could blame me for thinking that I have had enough of this life. If I could just close my eyes forever, this would all end. But I have not given in to those urges.

The main motivation for continuing, despite the struggles, is the ability to make further progress in research, lighting up the shadows of MND. I have always felt a strong compulsion to conduct MND research. It has been the thing that has motivated me to push through the darkest and hardest of days. But the engine that drives my compulsion has always been the family. More broadly, across the wider family I feel a kind of responsibility to keep working towards a therapy. We have already lost too many. More importantly, I promised my mother that I would do everything I could. I promised my sister Sarah that I would protect her kids. And I promised myself that I would keep working until I had used up every shred of energy I have. It has been the love of my family for me and my love for them that has been the fuel for my engine. If I felt that I could no longer contribute meaningfully to the field, I think that it would make this life harder to bear.

It would tip the scale.

That was the reality of what I was dealing with in 2019 when the funding ran out, and therapies that I thought showed the most promise had seemingly crumbled before my eyes. How could I continue to contribute in any meaningful way? I was struggling to see how. I could apply for funding for the following year, but that would make a twoyear gap in research projects, and that is assuming that I would even be successful next round. In reality, I would be less competitive next round, given the obvious downturn in productivity that would be the result of the gap in funding.

Let's get another thing straight. Living and working with a profound disability can be extremely challenging.

It is a titanic effort just to get me ready to be able to work every day, in that it takes about the same amount of time as a James Cameron film.

I use eye-gaze technology to painstakingly craft my applications. It takes ten times as long as an able-bodied person for me to put together an application. Nevertheless, I thought I would look over the failed application for funding to see if it could be improved.

I received a high score but just below the cut-off. I fell down in 'Publications'. The assessment of my published work can be summed up by the following from 'assessor 2': 'The track record was promising, however, relative to opportunity, I was looking for more first and last author publication.'

This made me mad. How could someone think that I could physically produce more than what I had done given my disability (and after scoring the impact of my work the highest score: 7). It made me wonder if I missed a part where I could explain my permanent disability.

No.

There was nowhere in the application to do this. This was a policy that applied in the same way for everybody but disadvantaged someone with a disability. Textbook discrimination. I asked the NHMRC to look at the guidelines and to have another look at my application in light of the inadequacies in making a reasonable adjustment. In response, the NHMRC updated their policy to allow a full explanation of circumstances and their impact on outputs in future applications. BUT, they determined that due process had been followed (i.e. assessors followed the existing guidelines when assessing my application). So they were happy because policy was followed. The very policy that discriminated against me and that they changed in response to my letter. By now, I was tired of fighting but I thought I'd ask other academics with a disability how they felt about the process. I got responses like:

'The impact disabilities have on our careers don't seem to come into consideration.'

'Most assessors would not understand.'

'*Terrible* processes for acknowledging impacts of disability.'

'It doesn't seem to make a difference.'

    I wrote to the NHMRC and to the Health Minister Greg Hunt MP about what I felt was a breach of the *Disability Discrimination Act* during my application for an investigator grant.

    Eventually, Anne Kelso, chief executive of the NHMRC, agreed with me. She said: 'As a result of Professor Justin Yerbury's correspondence, we have sought to make it clear that the impact of disability on the applicant's research output should be considered by peer reviewers.'

    I was awarded the funding and invited to contribute to the revised policy. In the next round explicit mention would be made of 'disability (including mental health conditions and psychosocial disability) or illness'.

    In the meantime, we received funding to properly test our combination therapy. We didn't know where the rumoured halting of the copper-ATSM clinical trial left us. We believed that the combination approach would provide additional benefit above and beyond what is possible with a single drug. Copper-ATSM has shown hints of promise in clinical trials to date, where it appears to slow disease progression. We hope that our combination will further slow the progression of MND and allow us to reduce the amount of copper-ATSM, which had been proving toxic at high doses. We need to be able to test for safety, maximum tolerated dose and efficacy. These are labour-intensive and expensive experiments. This would not be possible without FightMND and the generosity of the Australian public. So far our experiments have been encouraging. We have found that our combination delays symptom onset and extends the life of the MND mice. This has allowed us to reduce the amount of copper-ATSM used in order to limit its toxicity. Our goal now is to develop our combination therapy to a point where, if successful, we will be ready to move into clinical trials. There is a real optimism about the project within the team. We feel that we are moving forward and making real progress. However, we don't believe that it will be a cure. The best that we can hope for is that it slows down disease progression.

In July 2022, Biogen made a momentous announcement. They had submitted an application to the FDA for the use of the SOD1 antisense therapy for some cases of MND. The announcement of the submission came as a surprise given that even as recently as October 2021, a six-month Phase 3 randomised study did not meet the primary endpoint of change in the rate of disease progression. The new twelve-month study results showed that individuals who started treatment earlier experienced a decreased rate of decline in clinical and respiratory function, strength and an increased quality of life. What this tells me is that once the disease process has begun, it takes a lot to turn it around. MND is not a nimble and small speedboat. It is a large and unruly ship that is complex and diabolical to navigate. It makes sense to me that it takes a long time to turn this ship around. The earlier this therapy can be administered, the more effective it is likely to be. I predict that eventually the therapy will be able to be used prophylactically – well before symptoms start in people with a genetic risk of MND – so that the disease never gets a foothold.

This will be the first disease-modifying therapy that will be approved for use in MND. And it will hopefully herald a new era of drug discovery. Despite the fact that the new therapy has had a real impact on the progress of MND, we still believe that there is room for improvement. We continue to work on aspects of the delivery of therapies such as this antisense molecule with Kara and her team. We are particularly interested in making the therapy deliverable through the blood and also increasing the amount of drug that makes it into motor neurons.

The available data show that we are making real progress as a field, which has the potential to make a meaningful difference for people with MND. The worries that further research would be out of my reach back in 2019 turned out to be unfounded. The laboratory group is bigger and busier than it has ever been.

So what does that mean for me?

First we need to know who me is.

I have always found that I have compartmentalised aspects of my personality and that these go by different names. Justin is the son of Fred, and he is still trying to make his dad proud. Yerbs is the one who identifies most strongly with his physicality. He can be competitive to the point of aggressive, he would never back down from a fight and when he is with his mates, he drinks bourbon. Then there is J. He is a lover not a fighter. J is surrounded by women at home and work and is most comfortable in their company. J drinks coffee and red wine. There is also Dad and Uncle Justin, who is a big softie who is both nurturing and protective. Lastly there is the prof, who is quiet, introspective and logical. He never stops thinking.

For a long time, I thought I was essentially the same person but trapped in a seemingly lifeless body. I pleaded with Rachel to see past the paralysed and wasted limbs and the expressionless face. 'It is still me in here,' I would implore. But I cannot be the same person. How could I possibly be? MND has gouged, scratched and scraped at me to shape the person that I have become. While many of my personality traits have withered under the pressure of MND, the prof has flourished. While the physicality of self has been lost, my mind remains sharp. So I feel despite the 'slings and arrows of my outrageous fortune', I can still contribute. On balance, I still feel that I have enough to give, to outweigh the way I live. My mind is still active and I have a great team that I trust to test my ideas, and more and more of the team is coming up with their own ideas.

If I can hold on, I would like to be around to see MND beaten into submission. I would really like to see the dark corners of MND completely lit up so that there is no more mystery.

Like a giant eucalypt tree, MND casts a shadow so large that it is hard for anything to live under it. Those of us who have an inherited form of MND in the family and live our lives in its shadow typically have a choice between trying to find a little bit of light to nurture and warm us so that we might thrive in the shade or we wither in the unrelenting darkness. I have chosen not to be satisfied with finding some small patch of light coming dappled through the tangled mess of cover, but to use every last bit of my energy to burst a large enough hole through the canopy so that others too may be warmed by the sun. Perhaps one day, we will remove the tree altogether.

This is today's balancing act. How I feel tomorrow, next week or next year is another question altogether...

Although I have now convinced myself that I have lost parts of my personality and therefore relationships due to MND, telling this story has allowed me to come to the following conclusion. My sense of self is not irretrievably disintegrating. I don't think that MND is permanently killing off parts of my personality. I think that it would be impossible to continue in this endeavour without the fighting spirit of Yerbs, the love of J and the protectiveness of Dad and Uncle Justin.

Because I have been looking at this story under the microscope, I have been focused on only one thread of my story, and much of what has made up my humanity remains out of focus. All the little things that round out my story, which by themselves don't seem important but when added together make a life. And I did *live* in the years that I could. I experienced joy but also sadness. I felt jubilation but also pain. I made mistakes but I learned from them. I loved and was loved. And as I step into the twilight of my life, I have one thing left to leave you with and that is hope.

Acknowledgements

Writing this memoir has been harder and more rewarding than I could have ever imagined. None of this would have been possible without my wife, Rachel. She has stood by me during every struggle and all my successes. Rachel has put her own projects aside, not for the first time, to help me get this over the line. I'm forever indebted to Rachel for her editorial help, keen insight and ongoing support in bringing my stories to life. A big thank you also goes to Maddy for helping translate the science into an accessible language.

To my family, I am so thankful to have you in my life. To my dad for always being there, even during those dark and desperate years. To my daughters, Talia and Maddy, and their partners, Tyler and Alex: thank you for nothing but great memories. Thank you to my parents-in-law for your strength and unwavering support.

I wish to acknowledge the First Peoples of the Dharawal Country on which I live and work. I pay my respects to the traditional people and to the Elders past, present and emerging. I show my gratitude for their ongoing custodianship of the lands and oceans of the Illawarra.

To my many devoted friends from all over the world, I am fortunate to have you all on my side.

I'm eternally grateful to Amy and Gemma. Gemma, you took me seriously and gave me the courage to get started. A big thanks to Amy for your critical reading and for pushing the manuscript out into the world. It wouldn't be a book without you.

A very special thank you to Martin and the Affirm Press staff for believing in me and my story and for helping me to give voice to my words.

To my amazing research team, thank you for joining me in the fight against MND, not only for showing up every day to do the work but for your exceptional commitment and dedication to the cause, and for always going above and beyond. It's a privilege to work with you.

I appreciate the start in the research field that I was provided by Professor Mark Wilson, and the mentorship and international opportunities I was afforded by my dear friend and mentor Sir Professor Christopher Dobson FRS.

Thank you to the wider MND research community and my collaborators and friends at Cambridge University and the University of British Columbia, as well as multiple Australian universities – you know who you are, and I know who you are.

I am grateful to the multiple philanthropists who have helped to maintain my MND research in the lab, as well as the multiple funding bodies, including the MNDRIA and FightMND, who have always supported our work.

To everyone at the University of Wollongong, I'm honoured to be a part of this great educational institute. I appreciate the support of the vice-chancellors, which has enabled me to continue to work productively on my research.

Thank you to Professor Dominic Rowe for fighting for me and facilitating the extension of my life. The past six years of my life have been filled with many struggles, not least of all the struggle to get up and to face each day. This momentous task wouldn't have been possible if not for the tremendous help and care from my team of dedicated support workers and nurses, as well as various medical and allied health professionals.

For the people who have lived experience of MND, both those living with MND and their loved ones and carers, I hope this book helps others learn what it's like to Never Give Up.

Lastly, I want to thank the Wollongong community of which I have been a part for so long; thank you for showing up to watch me play in the Illawarra Hawks, for supporting my research and for recognising my achievements.

Notes and Resources

You have probably already guessed that the story that I have just told you is not the full picture. I have attempted to get the story across without getting too bogged down in every detail. However, I think that the detail, while not essential for the narrative of the book, is important in my life. For example, while I have mentioned around a dozen or so family members that have had MND, the reality of the devastation for our family is that over seventy people have died from this disease in the last hundred years.

I have also not described in any detail what my care team does for me every day. My support workers and nurses help me with every aspect of my daily care and medical needs, so that I can live my life. But it is not just that – these are humans who show compassion, care and skill to ensure that I can maintain my dignity and power, as much as possible.

Also, I have only discussed small fractions of the work undertaken by my dedicated team of researchers in my lab at the University of Wollongong.

In their own words...

At the University of Wollongong, Justin Yerbury continues to lead a research group dedicated to studying the molecular mechanisms that underpin amyotrophic lateral sclerosis. Justin's research in this field has contributed significantly to our understanding of the role misfolded and aggregated protein plays in the neuronal cell death associated with ALS.

Today, Justin's research team is tackling ALS from multiple angles: investigating how and why protein aggregation occurs, what makes it so toxic to motor neurons in particular, and searching for strategies to preserve motor neuron health. Many members of Justin's team knew him in the years prior to 2016, when his ALS was diagnosed. While their efforts focus on SOD1-associated familial ALS mutations, the team's work may uncover mechanisms that can be applied to the benefit of both sporadic and familial ALS.

Originally joining Justin's research team as an undergraduate student in 2011, Dr Luke McAlary has been fascinated by protein aggregation dynamics and pathogenesis ever since. Along with research assistant Victoria Shephard, Luke examines the instability of the proteins that coaggregate in ALS deposits, such as SOD1 and TDP-43. PhD candidate Vanessa Hollingsworth is investigating the role of another ALS associated protein, FUS, while PhD candidate Thomas Walker is examining protein phase separation and cellular stress responses to unfolded proteins.

Senior research assistant Natalie Farrawell joined Justin's research group in 2013 and plays a role in most projects across the laboratory. Natalie's particular focus is understanding how the cellular system that identifies, tags and removes misfolded proteins becomes overwhelmed in ALS, leading to motor neuron cell death.

A long-time friend of Justin's, Christen Chisholm, returned to research in 2019 to undertake her PhD studies in his laboratory. Christen is developing a genetic therapy designed to reduce the toxic accumulation of misfolded protein in motor neurons. Working alongside research assistants Dr Jody Gorman and Dr Rachael Bartlett, in collaboration with Canadian biotechnology company ProMIS, their strategy aims to enhance the cell's ability to break down the misfolded SOD1 protein via its own degradation machinery.

To address the lack of effective treatment options for ALS, Dr Jeremy Lum joined Justin's team in 2019. He identifies and assesses drugs that can prevent the misfolding of toxic ALS-associated proteins and encourage folding into their intended states. Jeremy and research assistant Mikayla Brown use a combination approach, whereby several novel molecules are used together to reduce the toxic accumulation of unfolded or misfolded proteins. It is hoped that the promising results of these studies could lead to improved treatment options for patients in the near future.

Dr Isabella Lambert-Smith began her studies with Justin in 2012, exploring the dysfunction that ALS brings to the cell's protein balancing systems, and uncovering a protective gene, UBA1, that may help to preserve motor neuron health by supporting this machinery. However, since ALS patients will have lost as many as eighty per cent of their motor neurons by the time of their diagnosis, Isabella is also developing a novel treatment approach that seeks to regenerate and replace lost motor neurons from the body's own healthy cells, so that people with ALS may one day be able to regain muscle function.

Since 2021, research assistant Dr Tracey Berg has been working behind the scenes for Justin, managing the laboratory's day-to-day administration and supporting the team's research efforts. Tracey's priority is to enable Justin to focus his energy on the bigger picture of the team's ongoing ALS research.

***

The following videos feature Justin Yerbury explaining the science behind motor neurone disease:

Australian Museum, 'Professor Justin Yerbury AM – Winner, 2022 Eureka Prize for Scientific Research', YouTube, uploaded by Australian Museum, 27 July 2022, youtube.com/watch?v=03 CECMR64_M.

Investment NSW, 'PPSE 2022 Winner – Justin Yerbury', YouTube, uploaded by Investment

NSW, 9 November 2022, youtube.com/watch?v=tn8XFrPUfJU.

University of Wollongong, 'Justin Yerbury: Explaining the role of protein folding in the progression of motor neurone disease', YouTube, uploaded by University of Wollongong, 5 September 2014, youtube.com/watch?v=ZdQChSxFnJ8.

Yerbury, Justin, 'An Infectious Idea: How protein folding drives MND progression', Big Ideas Festival, University of Wollongong, 16 October 2019, youtube.com/watch?v=stB04TRuBmM.

'Proteins: the stuff of life and how it shapes our understanding of MND, UOW Knowledge Series, University of Wollongong, 2 May 2019, youtube.com/watch?v=stB04TRuBmM.

'Shape Shifters: The role of protein misfolding in the progression of motor neurone disease', Budding Ideas, University of Wollongong, 26 May 2014, youtube.com/watch?v=kMdUy3ootSs.

My cousins Jamie (left) and Ashley, with me in the middle, on our aunty Bub's horse at Young, New South Wales, around 1976. I was a very active child, dubbed 'Hurricane Justin' by my mother, and spent my time running around with my cousins and sisters.

Me with my mother, Pauline, and my sister Naomi. We were always a very close-knit family.

Playing basketball with the West Sydney Slammers team in the Continental Basketball Association league. Basketball was a refuge for me in my awkward teenage years and it became my dream to play in the National Basketball League.

Rachel and me at her Year 12 graduation, November 1992. We met on New Year's Eve 1991 and have been together ever since.

Posing with my brand-new Illawarra Hawks basketball kit. I signed with them to play in the NBL for the 1995 season.

Our wedding at Minnamurra River, New South Wales, 18 February 1995. My uncle Ken had been diagnosed with motor neurone disease (MND) a few months previously – the first of many in our family. From left: Rachel's parents, Harry and Helen Hoogendoorn; Rachel and me; my mum and dad, Pauline and Fred Yerbury.

Rachel and I welcoming our first daughter, Talia, at Wollongong Hospital in 1996.

My maternal grandmother, Nan Joyce Pettit, with our second daughter, Maddy, in 1998.

A family holiday to Barrington Tops National Park in 1999, with Maddy in my jacket and Talia seated.

Rachel, Talia, Maddy and me in 1999. By this stage I had lost a few members of my extended family to MND, but the disease was about to hit much closer to home.

Left to right: My ancestor George Winter (d. 1882 aged 66), My great-great grandmother Mary Ann Barker (d. 1930 aged 44), My great-grandmother Daphne Abrahams (d. 1961 aged 53).

Some of the members of my extended family who have died from motor neurone disease.

The last photo of the Pettit family all together. Of the eight siblings, all but my uncle Bruce carried the SOD1 gene and have died from MND, as did my grandmother. Standing left to right: my mother, Pauline (d. 2002 aged 52), and her siblings Ken (d. 1995 aged 43), Susanne (d. 2011 aged 57), Bruce, Kathy (d. 2002 aged 44), Debbie (d. 2020 aged 62), Gay (d. 2009 aged 48) and Bub (d. 2020 aged 57). Seated: My grandfather Alan, and my grandmother Joyce (d. 2002 aged 72).

My cousins Stacey (d. 2006 aged 28) and Ashley (d. 1996 aged 21).

My sister Sarah (d. 2008 aged 26), pictured here with me.

A trip to Disneyland California in November 2007, after my sister Sarah had been diagnosed with MND. Standing: Rachel, Maddy, me, Talia, Jayson (Sarah's husband). Seated: Logan, Hannah and Sarah.

When I discovered that my family had a rare inherited form of MND, I made it my mission to search for a cure. Here I am at my PhD graduation in 2008 with Elise Stewart (friend and colleague, left) and my supervisor, Professor Mark Wilson.

I was awarded an Australian Research Council fellowship and spent almost a year at Cambridge University in 2009, so we took the opportunity to travel around Europe. In this photo, Maddy, Talia and I are leaping off the Caldera in Santorini, Greece.

In the lab at the University of Wollongong.

After my first symptoms of MND appeared in 2016, I continued to live my life as fully as I could. This trip to Africa in 2017 was our last big family adventure. Here, Maddy, Rachel, Talia and I watch the sunset across the Okavango Delta, Botswana.

In 2017 I had the opportunity to return to Cambridge, a place that held so many fond memories for me. In this photo I'm walking from Cambridge to Grantchester – my last big walk.

St John's College Master's Lodge at Cambridge University in 2017, with Sir Professor Christopher Dobson, who was so influential on my career.

A highlight of my last trip to Cambridge in 2017 was visiting Professor Stephen Hawking, a brilliant scientist and one of the most famous people with MND, at his Cambridge home. From left: Rachel, me, Sir Professor Christopher Dobson, Professor Stephen Hawking, Maddy and Talia.

Being awarded the Betty Laidlaw Award at the Australian MND symposium for outstanding mid-career researcher in November 2017.

By the end of 2017 my condition had declined significantly and I required noninvasive ventilation. Here I am at home with my faithful friend, Fern.

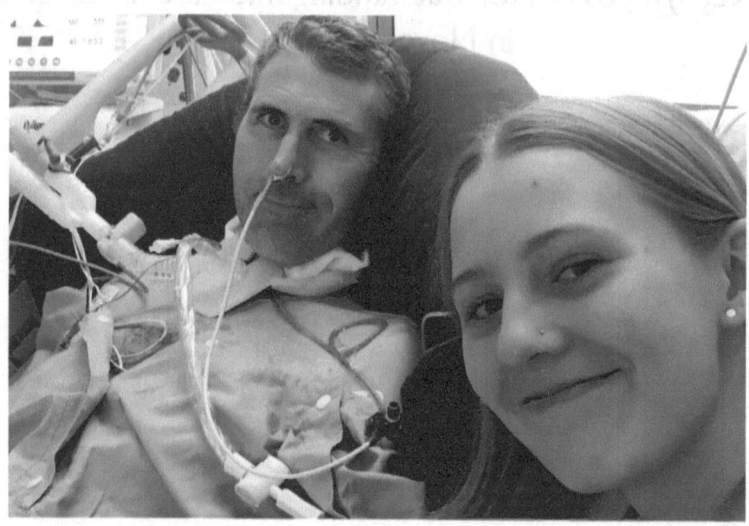

February 2018 at Macquarie University Hospital with Maddy after my life-extending laryngectomy surgery, after which I was no longer able to talk.

Talia and Tyler's wedding in our front yard, COVID-style, in March 2020. From left: Tyler, Talia, Justin, Rachel, Maddy, Alex.

At New South Wales Government House, Sydney, in September 2017, after receiving my Member of the Order of Australia award, with Maddy and Rachel.

Maddy has followed my footsteps into the world of science. She graduated with a Bachelor of Science from the University of Wollongong in 2022. From left: my dad, Maddy, me, Rachel's mum and Rachel.

At the awards ceremony for the 2022 Eureka Prizes, where I won the University of New South Wales prize for Scientific Research for my work on understanding the molecular causes of MND. Image courtesy of the Australian Museum.

At New South Wales Government House after receiving the New South Wales Premier's Award award for Excellence in Medical Biological Sciences in the 2022 NSW

Premier's Prizes for Science and Engineering. From left: Justin, Fred Yerbury (my dad), Rachel, and Her Excellency the Honourable Margaret Beazley, Governor of New South Wales.

Christmas with family. Back row from left: Tyler, Talia, Maddy, Jayson (Hannah and Logan's dad), Steve (Naomi's husband), Logan (Sarah's son), Fred (my dad), Alex, Naomi (my sister). Middle row from left: Archie and Morrison (Naomi and Steve's sons), Hannah (Sarah's daughter), Jenna (Jayson's wife). Front: Rachel, me, Sonny (Naomi and Steve's son).

Back Cover Material

Justin Yerbury made a promise to his mother while she was dying of motor neurone disease (MND) that he would do everything he could to find a cure. MND had already taken several members of Justin's family, and he learned that they carried a rare genetic form of the disease that gave them a fifty-fifty chance of inheritance.

Desperate to help his loved ones, Justin went to university to study science, eventually becoming a professor of molecular biology at the University of Wollongong and one of the world's leading experts on MND. While in New York, delivering a lecture on his groundbreaking research, Justin felt his thumb stop working – 'the beast' that had lurked so long in the shadows had caught up with him.

Now 99 per cent paralysed and able to move only his eyeballs, Justin refuses to yield. With eye-tracking software, he has written his extraordinary memoir to shine a light on this terrible disease and to show that, even in the bleakest of moments, there is always a reason to keep fighting.

All proceeds from this book will be donated to Fight MND.

www.ingramcontent.com/pod-product-compliance
Lightning Source LLC
Chambersburg PA
CBHW010717300426
44114CB00022B/2887